Beader's Stash

**Designs from
America's Favorite
Bead Shops**

Laura Levaas

 INTERWEAVE PRESS

Acknowledgments

Special thanks to: Linda Ligon, Linda Stark, Marilyn Murphy, Betsy Armstrong, Rebecca Campbell, Anne Merrow, Danielle Fox, Dustin Wedekind, Jamie Hogsett, Marlene Blessing, Paulette Livers, Pauline Brown, Dean Howes, Nancy Arndt, Bonnie Hoover, and Ann Swanson. Extra special thanks to project editor Melinda A. Barta, technical editor and illustrator Bonnie Brooks, Brian Adamo, and my family for their encouragement and unfailing patience.

Text © 2006, Interweave Press LLC
Illustration © 2006, Interweave Press LLC
Photography © 2006, Interweave Press LLC

 Interweave Press LLC
201 East Fourth Street
Loveland, CO 80537–5655 USA
www.interweave.com

Printed in Singapore by Imago
Library of Congress Cataloging-in-Publication Data

Levaas, Laura, 1975-
  Beader's stash : designs from America's favorite bead shops / Laura Levaas, author.
     p. cm.
  Includes index.
  ISBN 13: 978-1-931499-80-4 (pbk.)
  ISBN 10: 1-931499-80-2 (pbk.)
  1. Beadwork. I. Title.
  TT860.L47 2006
  745.58'2--dc22   2006005250

10 9 8 7 6 5 4 3 2 1

Contents

Projects by Type

Editor's Introduction

by Laura Levaas

I treasure my bead stash. It had humble beginnings, assembled from a mishmash of round plastic beads from a broken bracelet and some store-bought glass seed beads. Even before I knew much about the world of beading, I was drawn to beads—their shapes, colors, textures, the sheer variety. Through my job with Interweave Press and *Beadwork* magazine, I've been lucky to travel to dozens of bead shows and shops, and my stash has grown sizably . . . although it's not much better organized than when I first started! In five years of working in the world of beads, I've observed one trait common to beaders: their willingness to share new ideas and inspiration about the craft. Their enthusiasm is infectious.

In assembling the projects for this book, I made contact with bead shop owners from many walks of life. Some have been in the business more than twenty years, while some opened their bead shops just a few years ago. Many run thriving Web and mail-order companies; others make their living through loyal customers and walk-in business. But all were eager to communicate their knowledge and ideas about the craft of beading. And that's what makes *Beader's Stash* special—it's a collection of patterns that showcases the wisdom of America's bead stores.

Over a year ago, we wrote to bead shops in the United States and Canada, asking for their most favorite and sought-after designs and inspirational projects—the ones that sent their customers running for their beads. We were overwhelmed by the response: nearly ninety bead shops (all of which are listed in the Honor Roll and Directory pages of this book) submitted more than 300 projects for consideration. A panel of jurors from *Beadwork* magazine, Interweave Press's book publishing team, and other beading experts chose the projects (in a "blind" selection process) they felt were the best and most creative use of color, texture, and technique.

Making final selections wasn't easy, so we did our best to choose projects that would appeal to all levels of beaders and represent many different categories of beadwork. The projects here include dressy and casual jewelry, fun home décor, and other accessories that show creative uses of beads on clothing. Most projects require materials readily available at your local bead shop or chain store; we've provided contact information for finding some of the specialty beads and materials called for in projects or feel free to contact the sponsoring shops directly for more information. You may not always be able to find the exact type of bead featured in a project so get creative, experiment with the beads in your stash, or head to your favorite bead shop for that perfect substitute bead.

Going on a road trip? Let the bead shops listed in the Directory guide you across the country! We've also included a handy "Beading Basics" section at the end of the book—go there first if you need a refresher course or want to learn a new technique. Scattered throughout the book you'll find dozens of helpful tips that were submitted by most of our participating bead shops.

Flip through the pages of *Beader's Stash* and be inspired to rediscover your own stash of beads. If you are like me and always need that finishing touch to top off your stash, indulge yourself with a trip to your local bead shop for a perfect toggle clasp, just the right shade of seed bead, or even a few words of encouragement.

Happy beading.

Bead Shop Honor Roll

For at least one month prior to the submission deadline for *Beader's Stash*, the front offices of Interweave Press overflowed with potential projects for this book. Selecting thirty-nine designs from over 300 submissions was exciting but challenging—imagine seeing all that beadwork spread out in one room! We express our sincerest thanks to the bead shops listed here for sending their projects because without them this book would not have been possible.

We encourage you to explore the bead shops in your region and beyond, especially during your travels, to see the projects and techniques we weren't able to include here. See for yourself what they have to offer.

*Alaska Bead Company	Anchorage, Alaska
*Albion Beads	Wakefield, Massachusetts
*Ambrosia Bead Company	Yakima, Washington
Bead Angels Bead Shop	Indianapolis, Indiana
*Bead Bin	Madison, Wisconsin
*Bead Cache, The	Fort Collins, Colorado
*Bead Culture	Jackson, Michigan
Bead Depot Etc.	Tehachapi, California
Bead Dreams	Orlando, Florida
*Bead Factory, The	Tacoma, Washington
Bead Gallery Inc.	Salem, New Hampshire
Bead Garden, The	Bainbridge Island, Washington
Bead Garden, The	Silverdale, Washington
Bead Haven	Cedar Rapids, Iowa
*Bead in Hand	Oak Park, Illinois
Bead Me Up!	Apple Valley, Minnesota
Bead Museum, The	Glendale, Arizona
*Bead Shop, The	Palo Alto, California
Bead Tree, The	West Falmouth, Massachusetts
*Bead Works Inc.	Franklin, Michigan
Beadazzled	Washington, D.C.
Beadazzled	Baltimore, Maryland
Beadazzled	Cary, North Carolina
Beadazzled	McLean, Virginia
Beadcats/Universal Synergetics	Wilsonville, Oregon
*Beadclub	Woodinville, Washington
Beadecked Bead Shoppe	Southington, Connecticut
Beadful Things	North Fort Myers, Florida
*Beadin' Path, The	Freeport, Maine
Beading Place, The	Tustin, California
*Beadissimo	San Francisco, California
Beadoholique Bead Shop	Spring, Texas
Beadoholique Too!	Houston, Texas
*Beads & Beyond	Bellevue, Washington
*Beads by Design	Marietta, Georgia
*Beads of Colour	Dundas, Ontario, Canada
Beads of Marin Inc.	Mill Valley, California
*Beauty and the Beads Inc.	Santa Fe, New Mexico
Blue Santa Beads	Media, Pennsylvania
*Bluewater Beads Inc.	Online only
*Boca Loca Beads Inc.	Indianapolis, Indiana
Brighton Beads and More	Brighton, Michigan
Buttons, Bangles & Beads	St. Pete Beach, Florida
*Castleander Beads & Crafts	Hudson, New Hampshire
Creative Castle	Newbury Park, California
*Creative Fringe LLC, The	Grand Haven, Michigan

Dana Rudolph and Company	Troy, New York
Dava Bead and Trade	Portland, Oregon
EZBeads.com	Chadds Ford, Pennsylvania
Farrin O'Connor Design Studios	Pasadena, California
*Galena Bead Bar, The	Galena, Illinois
General Bead	San Francisco, California
General Bead	National City, California
Gig's Beads 'N Things	Homer, Alaska
Gossamer Wings Beads	La Crosse, Wisconsin
Heart Bead	Kneeland, California
Hole Affair, The	Jackson, California
*Holy Crow Beads	Clarksburg, Ontario, Canada
Insomniac Beads LLC	Plymouth, Minnesota
*International Glass & Bead Company	Claremont, California
*Lady Bug Beads	St. Louis, Missouri
Land of Odds/Be Dazzled Beads	Nashville, Tennessee
Legendary Beads	Santa Rosa, California
*Magpies Inc.	Cherry Valley, Illinois
*Meant to Bead	Toledo, Ohio
*Nordic Gypsy Beads and Jewelry	Rochester, Minnesota
*Ornamentea	Raleigh, North Carolina
*Planet Bead	Hillsboro, Oregon
*Poppy Field Bead Company	Albuquerque, New Mexico
Purple Mountain Beads	Fort Collins, Colorado
Rainbow House	Aniak, Alaska
Regal Beader	Muskegon, Michigan
*Saki Silver	Cincinnati, Ohio
*San Gabriel Bead Company, The	Arcadia, California
*Sorrelli	Sheridan, Wyoming
Star's Beads Ltd.	Vienna, Virginia
*String Beads	Salt Lake City, Utah
Studio Baboo	Charlottesville, Virginia
*Suzie Q Beads	Calgary, Alberta, Canada
*Sweet Beads	Minnetonka, Minnesota
Talisman Beads	Eureka, California
*Third Eye Beads & Gift Gallery	San Clemente, California
Timeless Treasures Inc.	Montclair, New Jersey
*Turquoise/String Beads	Fall River, Massachusetts
Urban Girl	Bismarck, North Dakota
Yellow Brick Road	Dublin, Ireland

*Projects from these shops are featured in this book.

5

Textured Links Necklace

● ● ● ● ● ● ● ● ● ● ● ● ● ● ● ● ● ●

Gail Piper

A sterling silver necklace made of small and large interlocking circles inspired Gail, an artist and teacher, to create this energetic piece. Sterling silver crimp bead covers are integrated into the links to disguise many of the closed crimp tubes. Use memory wire for the last link to conceal the closure, and to mix it up add drops, triangles, cubes, and crystals to vary the textures.

Materials
  3 g mauve AB size 11° Czech seed beads (A)
  3 g amber AB size 11° Czech seed beads (B)
  1 g black size 11° Czech seed beads (C)
  6 g mauve matte AB 4×3mm Japanese
    teardrops (D)
  6 g black AB 3×2mm Japanese teardrops (E)
  2 g mauve matte size 2° Japanese bugles
  2 g mauve AB glass size 10° Japanese triangles
  30 gray AB 3mm Swarovski crystal bicones (F)
  40 purple 3mm Swarovski crystal bicones (G)
  27 sterling silver 3mm round beads
  18 sterling silver 3mm crimp covers

  60 sterling silver 1×1mm crimp tubes
  2¾" (7 cm) of ring size memory wire
  150" (3.8 m) of .014 beading wire

Tools
  Chain-nose pliers
  Round-nose pliers
  Wire cutters

Techniques
  Crimping, stringing

Finished Size
  21" (53.5 cm)

TIP Work Ahead

✔ Once you complete a full sequence of links (as in Steps 1–5 of this project), use the links that you have finished as a visual guide. Once the pattern is apparent, it is easy to see which links you can make up ahead. It's easiest to skip every other link and make just one or two links. Many find it easier to pull the wire tight and trim the wires close without the weight of the completed links in the way.

—Bead Bin

---

this project is from
Bead Bin

414 Westgate Mall
Madison, WI 53711
(608) 274-0104

When Bead Bin opened in 1994, it featured just enough space for a glass display case, a cash register, and two walls of hooks for beads. Students even used television trays during beading classes because there wasn't enough room for a table. The shop is now four times larger, offering ample elbow room, aisle space, and freedom to appreciate the myriad colors and textures.

Owner Chris Schneider believes that starting out with a tiny bead shop taught her to organize her space, a skill she still uses in the expanded store. The selection—crystals, gold, silver, glass, gemstones, Czech and Japanese seed beads, lampworked beads, charms, and findings—can be found in neat, organized rows on shelves.

Bead Bin offers a variety of classes throughout the year, from basic stringing, wireworking, and earring courses to more advanced beadweaving techniques. Although the days of television trays are over, Chris likes to keep the class sizes small. "We have great teachers and small class sizes because we want students to be successful in their attempts, not frustrated," she says. "Our staff loves working here, and it shows in their enthusiasm and willingness to share their knowledge."

Visit Bead Bin for a full selection of beads, stringing materials, books, tools, and exciting classes in a friendly, easy-to-shop atmosphere.

Textured Links Necklace variation

Step 1: Using the end of the wire from the spool, string 1 crimp tube, *1 triangle, 8As, and 1 silver round bead. Repeat from * once then string 1 triangle and 8As. Run the wire through the crimp tube, pull tight, flatten the crimp tube, and trim the wire close. Cover the flattened crimp tube with one crimp cover and set aside. Make a second circle of beads in the same manner: String 1 crimp tube, 21As, run the wire through the crimp tube, pull tight, flatten the crimp tube, and trim the wire close. Cover the flattened crimp tube with a crimp cover. These two links will be treated as one when combining them in the necklace throughout this project.

Step 2: String 1 crimp tube. String 1D and 1B ten times. String 1D. Slip the wire through both of the two links created in Step 1, run the wire through the crimp tube, pull tight, flatten the crimp tube, and trim the wire close.

Step 3: String 1 crimp tube. String 1F and 8Bs three times. Slip the wire through the link created in Step 2, run the wire through the crimp tube, pull tight, flatten the crimp tube, and trim the wire close.

Step 4: String 1 crimp tube. String 1E and 1A ten times. String 1D. Slip the wire through the link created in Step 3, run the wire through the crimp tube, pull tight, flatten the crimp tube, and trim the wire close.

Step 5: String 1 crimp tube. String 1C, 1 bugle, 1C, and 1G four times. Slip the wire through the link made in Step 4. Run the wire through the crimp tube, pull tight, flatten the crimp tube, and trim the wire close.

Step 6: Repeat Steps 1–5 for a total of 20" (51 cm). For the clasp, create a small loop on one end of the memory wire using the round-nose pliers and string 1 silver bead, 5As, 1G, 8As, 1 silver bead, 8As, 1G, 8A, 1 silver bead, 7As, 1G, 7As, and 1 silver bead. Create a final turn at the end of the memory wire to hold the beads in place. Pass this clasp through the first and last links.

Opposites Attract

Debi Keir-Nicholson

Debi was immediately intrigued by needle felting, a dry, clean process that gives the artist complete control over shape, size, and color of the finished product. Debi's felted beads—with magnets cleverly embedded for a secure closure—were inspired by the artistry of felt jewelry maker Carol Huber Cypher. Experiment with an entire bracelet or necklace composed of felted beads.

Materials
  12 green 6mm glass rondelles
  10 red-lined amber resin 15×15mm barrels
  2 sterling silver 2×2mm crimp tubes
  11" (28 cm) of .024 beading wire
  2 cylinder-shaped 6×6mm earth magnets
  2 steel cups to fit the magnets
  .25 oz each of red and yellow wool fleece
  E6000 cement

Tools
  Felting needle
  Styrofoam block about 4×4×2" (10×10×5 cm)
    for work surface
  Soft Flex Speeder Beader for .024 wire

Techniques
  Needle felting, stringing, crimping, tension bead

Finished Size
  9" (23 cm) bracelet; 1" (2.5 cm) diameter each
    felt bead

Note: Magnets and cups are available from hardware stores or from online resources; fleece is available at your local yarn shop or from online resources.

TIP Needle Felting

✔ Be alert and be careful, as felting needles have very sharp barbs. If desired, protect your fingers by wearing leather thimbles. Consider using a tool comprised of multiple needles mounted in a wooden handle (sold with felting needles), to speed up the felting process.

—Beads of Colour

---

this project is from
Beads of Colour

65 Main St.
Dundas, ON, Canada L8N 2P9
(905) 628-6886
debi@beadsofcolour.com
www.beadsofcolour.com

Shoppers at Beads of Colour would never guess that proprietor Debi Keir-Nicholson was once told that she was "afraid of color." Bright banners line the entrance to the shop, cases overflow with sparkling stones and seed beads, and the walls simply drip with beads of every shade. "Color is mesmerizing," Debi says. "Symbolically, color represents life. Living life with enthusiasm is what feeds my creative energies."

Those creative energies, combined with a love of beads and a background in design, led her to open the store in 1997. Products range from colorful Miyuki, Toho, Czech, and Italian seed beads, to a diverse selection of semiprecious, vintage, hand-blown Murano, and other unusual beads from around the world, as well as furnace glass, loom-worked goods, findings, and finished jewelry.

Beads of Colour is the hub of an active beading culture. Ten instructors teach a variety of beading techniques throughout the year, the Upper Canada Bead Guild meets there monthly, and the shop hosts regular bead and jewelry swaps. Debi is one of the founding members of Dundas Studio Tour, where she presents her new work annually. Much of her art shows an international flair that evolved during years of traveling the globe and collecting beads.

The sense of community is strong at Beads of Colour, a fact Debi attributes in part to the history of the building, which over the years has been a coffee shop, handmade shoe shop, and bicycle shop. "I think there is always going to be a community in this building," she says. "Once you have that, people enjoy being part of it."

Felting

Step 1: Take a 6" (15 cm) strip of red fleece and roll it into a tight round ball, ¼" (6mm) larger than the finished bead size.

Step 2: Working carefully on top of the Styrofoam block, needle the ball with deep pokes, catching the loose ends and pushing them into the center of the ball. Frequently rotate the ball and continue to poke to make it round. If you need to increase the size of the ball to reach the finished size, wrap a thin layer of fleece around the ball and continue to rotate and needle to attach the fleece.

Step 3: Once the ball is round and the finished size is reached, continue poking in one spot to form a round depression that is large enough to fit one rondelle and one steel magnet cup. If needed, clean up the depression by poking any stray fibers or lumpy areas.

Step 4: Repeat Steps 1–3 using the yellow fleece for a second felted bead.

Stringing

Step 5: String 1 crimp tube and firmly crimp. Attach the needle to the wire and string 1 rondelle (this will serve as a tension bead). String the wire through the center of the depression of one bead, through the felt bead, and exit on the other side. Pull hard until the rondelle and crimp sit inside the depression.

Step 6: Coat the outside of the steel cup with cement and with the cup opening facing out, press into the depression.

Step 7: String 1 rondelle and 1 barrel ten times. String 1 rondelle and pass the needle through the second felt bead, this time from the round side and exiting out the center of the depression. String 1 rondelle and 1 crimp tube. Crimp the end of the wire so that the crimp tube is sitting tightly in the depression. Cement the second steel cup with the cup opening facing out in the second felt bead.

Step 8: Cement one magnet in each steel cup.

VARIATION The dark-colored bead is made of green fleece and covered with very thin lines of yellow fleece. The light-colored bead is made of tan fleece, circled with small stripes of red and yellow fleece and yellow, white, and light green disks of fleece. To add these decorative elements, roll a 2" (5 cm) long piece of fleece between your fingers to make a stripe or form a small piece of fleece into a disk to make a dot. Insert the felting needle into the edge of one of the shapes to catch the fleece in the barbs of the needle, and stab the needle into the center of the bead. Without completely withdrawing the needle, secure the fleece further by repeatedly stabbing the shapes.

Opposites Attract variation

"A bead shop isn't like a grocery store," says String Beads owner Dinah Ihle. Clearly thrilled to operate a store where people shop because they enjoy themselves and their craft, not because they consider it a chore, Dinah has created a store where customer service is key. A beader and art glass designer, she opened String Beads twelve years ago with the aim of creating a store to meet the needs and anticipate the desires of any beader.

String Beads offers a variety of classes every week, ranging from color theory and beadweaving techniques to stringing and wireworking. Customers find a huge selection of beads, stones, metals, and findings, as well as lampworked beads, fused glass, and wearable beaded art, some of which is sold and shown nationally. The emphasis on customer service extends through the store's back office, where co-owner Bob Ihle drew on his background in engineering and small business management to create itemized sales receipts for shoppers and streamlined inventory tracking to keep items in stock.

"We're all really lucky that people walk in our doors," Dinah says. "We enjoy our customers. And if you can teach someone something, you're having a good time!" Whether it's extra personal attention like helping a novice beader learn a new technique or demonstrating how to use the tools at the worktable, each of String Beads's nine staff members takes time to make every customer happy. "We take pride in what we do," says Dinah.

Ice Trap Lariat

Roxanne Vigos

String Beads designer Roxanne captures the beauty and complexity of ice crystals in this frosty-looking lariat. Crystal and glass pearls, quartz chips, and silver-lined seed beads are "trapped" in place by the lariat's pewter bail. This must-have accessory is a gorgeous addition to any winter apparel but could also cool down the hottest summer attire.

Materials
 10 g clear silver-lined size 11° Japanese seed beads
 16 clear 12mm Swarovski crystal faceted rounds
 1 clear foil-lined 9mm round bead
 115 clear 5–12mm quartz chips
 2 white 4mm Swarovski crystal pearls
 7 white 8mm Swarovski crystal pearls
 1 white 16mm Swarovski crystal pearl
 2 silver 10×8mm faceted rondelles
 5 Bali silver 4mm daisy spacers
 1 Bali silver 7×4mm spacer
 1 Bali silver 6×10mm charm
 1 pewter bead cap to fit 16mm pearl
 1 pewter 16×24mm bail
 1 pewter 6×30mm tube
 3 sterling silver 2×2mm crimp tubes
 54" (137 cm) of .014 beading wire

Tools
 Crimping pliers
 Wire cutters

Techniques
 Stringing, crimping

Finished Size
 28" (71 cm)

Step 1: Set aside five 12mm crystals, one 8mm pearl, two 4mm pearls, three 4mm daisy spacers, 30–35 crystal chips, the tube, and the charm to make the Ice Drop sections below the bail in Steps 4–5.

Step 2: Find the center of the wire and adjust so that one side is 3" (7.5 cm) longer than the other and fold the wire. String 3 size 11°s, the bail, and 3 size 11°s on one end. Move the beads to the fold, string both ends through 1 crimp tube and crimp. (Figure 1.)

Step 3: String both ends through the 16mm pearl, bead cap, 1 silver rondelle, one 7×4mm spacer, and one 12mm crystal. Separate the two strands. *Working in a random pattern for 2–2¼" (5–5.5 cm) on each strand, string size 11°s, chips, daisy spacers, 12mm crystals, and 8mm pearls. String both ends through one 12mm crystal. Repeat from * until the section measures at least 15" (38 cm). (Figure 2.)

Figure 1

Figure 2

Step 4: String both ends through 1 silver rondelle and 1 daisy spacer, one end through
12 size 11°s, the other end through 6 chips,
and both ends through the foil-lined bead.
String the two wire cables through the bail
and begin to make the Ice Drops.

Step 5: *Ice Drops.* String 1" (2.5 cm) of size
11°s, add small sections of crystal chips
between more size 11°s at random on the
short end of the wire for 7¼" (18.5 cm).
Working with the short end, string one
4mm pearl, the metal tube, 1 crimp tube,
one 4mm pearl, one 12mm crystal, and 1
size 11°. Pass back through the 12mm crystal, 4mm pearl, and crimp tube. Crimp,
pulling the wire tight before crimping so the
crimp tube will be hidden inside the tube;
trim the wire close.

Step 6: String the beads and chips as in Step
5 on the long end of the wire for 7½"
(19 cm). String one 12mm crystal, 2 chips,
1 daisy spacer, one 8mm pearl, 1 daisy spacer,
2 chips, one 12mm crystal, and 1 size 11°
two times. String one 12mm crystal, 1 crimp
tube, and the charm. Pass back through the
crimp tube and crimp; trim the wire close.

Bohemian Breeze Lantern

Dara Spiotto

Dara, the former West Coast sales representative for The Beadin' Path, has been teaching beadwork for the past seven years. Her lantern is a great representation of her love of fringe and how beads don't always have to be used for personal adornment. Aside from how beautiful the beads look, they also sound wonderful when they brush past one another, especially if you use hollow metal beads or bells like the pink and orange variation. Hang in a sunny window, near a bright lamp, or where a gentle breeze can turn the lantern into a subtle wind chime.

Materials
247 assorted green, brown, amber, cream, and copper 3–25mm resin, glass, metal, and crystal beads
20 sterling silver 1×2mm crimp tubes
10' (3 m) of .019 beading wire
10' (3 m) of green waxed linen cord
1 metal ring 3" (7.5 cm) in diameter

Tools
Wire cutter
Crimping pliers
3 alligator clips
Scissors
Permanent marker

Techniques
Stringing, crimping, knotting, fringe

Finished Size
14" (35.5 cm)

Note: Metal rings are available at craft stores or from online resources.

Fringe

Step 1: Cut the wire into ten 12" (30.5 cm) pieces. Working with one wire, string 1 crimp tube, wrap the wire around the ring, pass the end of the wire back through the crimp tube, and crimp. String assorted beads for 9½" (24 cm), 1 crimp tube, and 1 small bead, pass back through the crimp tube, and crimp; trim the wire close.

TIP Work Ahead

✔ If you wish to use beads larger than 25mm, consider making fewer fringes so that the beads hang freely without touching each other. If you wish to lay out the beads in a zigzag pattern in your fringe, use an even number of beads because using an odd number will make it difficult to come out with a balanced pattern.

—The Beadin' Path

---

this project is from

The Beadin' Path

15 Main St.
Freeport, ME 04032
(207) 865-4785
beads@beadinpath.com
www.beadinpath.com

The Beadin' Path in Freeport, Maine, caters to beaders looking for the unusual and eclectic. Packed with inspiration, this welcoming shop is owned by the mother-and-daughter team of Jan Parker and Heather DeSimone. Originally a 400-square-foot space, the shop has grown to 4,500 square feet of beader's paradise.

The Beadin' Path specializes in vintage Swarovski crystals, German glass beads, and Lucite beads, along with a range of stones, pearls, Japanese seed beads, and an extensive lampwork collection. Shoppers can visit the website to browse online specials, sign up for the newsletter, or register for "Beads in the Mail," a monthly shipment of beads that are not yet available in the store. "We all truly love beads," Heather says. "Everyone who works here is eager to show off the latest shipments, the newest artists, or the one little treasure they put aside just for that special customer."

Employees of The Beadin' Path are an extension of the owners' family, each adding their unique talents to the business. Staff members enjoy taking time to share new ideas and work on projects brought in by visitors. And if you don't have a project in mind, let the variety of classes inspire you. Classes reflect the tastes of this creative group and include topics like knotting, stringing basics, beadweaving, rings, amulet bags, wireworking, tassels, and more. "Beads bring people together," Heather says. "We're happy to be at the hub of that for our local community."

Step 2: Repeat Step 1 nine times, following the established pattern.

Step 3: Lay the ring down flat, spread out the bead strands so that they are evenly spaced, and mark their placement with the marker. *Wrap the cord tightly around the ring until you reach a marked line and slide one strand of beads to the line. Repeat from * nine times. Wrap the ring until it is covered.

Top

Step 4: Cut the cord into three 8" (20.5 cm) pieces. Tie the end of one piece of cord to the ring, string assorted beads for 2¾" (7 cm), and place an alligator clip on the end of the cord.

Step 5: Repeat Step 4 two times, following the established pattern and equally spacing the cords around the ring, about 3¼" (8.5 cm) apart.

Step 6: Remove the alligator clips and use all three cords to string assorted beads with large holes for 2¾" (7 cm). Using all three cords, tie one knot above the last bead and one knot ¼" (6 mm) from the ends.

Bohemian Breeze Lantern variation

Picture Perfect

● ● ● ● ● ● ● ● ● ● ● ●

Christine C. Griffith

A relatively new beader, Christine created this vintage-looking necklace using a photograph, microscope slides, copper foil tape, and a soldering iron. Although a beginner can master the necessary skills, the finished piece looks accomplished and sophisticated. Christine has strung pearls, crystals, and smoky topaz to accentuate the nostalgic feel of the antique photograph, which shows Kate Richbourg's grandmother. Try using vintage stamps or an original artwork in place of the photograph, insert two photographs back-to-back for a reversible pendant, or solder jump rings to both ends of the pendant for a horizontal jewelry component. Let your imagination run wild!

Materials
22 jet hematite 6mm Swarovski
   crystal bicones
164 peacock gray 4mm freshwater pearls
60 peacock gray 7mm freshwater pearls
4 smoky topaz 10×14mm faceted tablets
60 Bali silver 4mm daisy spacers
1 sterling silver 2-strand box clasp
4 sterling silver 2×2mm crimp tubes
2 black 5mm jump rings
62" (157.5 cm) of .014 beading wire
1 photograph or postcard 1×3" (2.5×7.5 cm)
2 glass 1×3" (2.5×7.5 cm) microscope slides
12" (30.5 cm) of 7⁄32" (6mm) wide
   copper foil tape
1⁄8" (3mm) in diameter wire solder
Soldering flux

Tools
Wire cutters
Crimping pliers
Flat-nose pliers
45-watt soldering iron with 1⁄8" (3mm) tip
Fireproof soldering brick
Small brush for flux
Burnisher
2 alligator clips

Techniques
Stringing, crimping, soldering

Finished Size
16" (40.5 cm)

Note: Materials are available at stained glass, craft, bead, and hardware stores or from online resources.

this project is from

Beadissimo

1051 Valencia St.
San Francisco, CA 94110
(415) 282-2323
info@beadissimo.com
www.beadissimo.com

"Anyone can be creative," says owner Kate Richbourg. "Our promise is interesting beads, creative ideas, and great value. We focus on unique beads and innovative classes, and hope to cultivate imagination and originality for a long time to come," adds co-owner Christine C. Griffith.

In 2003, Beadissimo opened its doors in San Francisco's colorful Mission District, located in a building that survived the earthquake and fire of 1906. Inside, Kate and Christine shake things up by offering cutting-edge products, excellent teachers, and unique classes. The most popular items include semiprecious, glass, and ethnic beads and pendants, although the shop also carries a wide assortment of seed beads, clasps, findings, and tools.

Classes range from basic stringing to bead crochet, chain making, fused metalwork, glass, jewelry design, metalworking, Precious Metal Clay, and wirework. A comprehensive website contains information on staff and instructors, extensive class descriptions and photographs, and recommended reading. Trunk shows keep customers up-to-date on the latest trends.

Beadissimo is more than a bead store, it's an experience. Cruise over to the lounge area, get cozy in a comfortable chair, and browse books and magazines for a spark of creativity. Once inspired, move over to the workstation, where you'll find tools and bead boards to help you get started creating.

Pendant

Step 1: Sandwich the photograph between both of the pieces of glass.

Step 2: Join the pieces of glass using the tape: starting in the middle of the bottom side, center the short end of the tape over the glass, fold the tape down over the edges (equal amounts of tape should be on both the front and back of the glass). Rotate the pieces of glass to cover all sides, making sure to neatly fold the corners of the tape. Using the burnisher and being careful not to tear the tape, completely burnish the tape so that it is securely adhered to the glass.

Step 3: Place the pendant faceup on the soldering brick and use the flux brush to lightly cover the tape with flux; excessive amounts of flux will burn while soldering.

Step 4: Cut the solder wire into ¼" (6 mm) pieces. Pick up one piece of the solder with the soldering iron and run the tip of the soldering iron, melting and spreading the solder, slowly down the tape. Solder all four of the edges that are facing up, covering the tape and picking up more pieces of solder as needed. When cool, turn the pendant over, apply more flux, and repeat the soldering process on the back edges. Turn the pendant to the side and repeat on the side edges.

Step 5: Touch the soldering iron to the center of the top of the pendant to melt the solder slightly and holding the jump ring in the flat-nose pliers, gently push the jump ring into place. When cool and using the flat-nose pliers, add the second jump ring to the first in the same manner so that the pendant hangs forward.

Necklace

Step 1: Cut a 28" (71 cm) piece of wire. String 2 spacers, eighty-two 4mm pearls, the pendant through the jump ring, and eighty-two 4mm pearls. Place an alligator clip on each end.

Step 2: Cut a 28" (71 cm) piece of wire. String 1 crimp tube, 1 spacer, *1 more spacer, three 7mm pearls, 1 spacer, 1 crystal, 2 spacers, 1 crystal, 1 spacer, five 7mm pearls, 1 spacer, 1 crystal, 2 spacers, 1 crystal, 1 spacer, three 7mm pearls, 1 spacer, and 1 tablet. Repeat from *. String 1 spacer, three 7mm pearls, 1 spacer, 1 crystal, 2 spacers, 1 crystal, 1 spacer, five 7mm pearls, 1 spacer, 1 crystal, 1 spacer, and the pendant through the jump ring.

Step 3: Mirror the pattern established in Step 2.

Step 4: Twist both strands together and crimp each strand to the clasp; trim the wires close.

Black Tie Affair and Green Apple Glitz Martini Sticks

Lea Worcester

Lea is known as the master of wireworking at Sweet Beads. Her increasingly popular martini sticks class is a fun way for students to use up odd beads in their bead stash, and they walk away with quick and easy handmade gifts. Try them as hat pins and party picks, or even place them in the base of a plant for a little touch of glitz.

Materials for Black Tie Affair
8 clear foil-lined size 8mm round beads
8 sterling sliver 2.5mm round beads
8 black 7×3mm faceted flat round beads
4 black 9×13mm faceted teardrops
4 silver 6mm star charms
7" (18 cm) of sterling silver 18-gauge
   dead-soft square wire
4 metal 6" (15 cm) long pins

Materials for Green Apple Glitz
4 green 4mm round beads
4 green foil-lined 6mm round beads
4 amber lampworked 8mm round beads
4 amber foil-lined 10×13mm chiclets
8 peridot 6mm Swarovski crystal
   square rondelles

4 sterling silver 2.5mm round beads
4 metal 6" (15 cm) long pins

Tools
Wire cutters
Round-nose pliers
Chain-nose pliers
Medium-fine nail file
Washcloth
G-S Hypo Cement
Toothpick

Technique
Wireworking

Finished Size
6" (15 cm)

⭐ **TIP** Stabilizing Beads with Large Holes

✔ To prevent large-holed beads from wobbling on your stringing wire or cord, consider adding a 4–6mm crystal bicone on each side of the large-holed bead. About half of each bicone will be hidden inside the large-holed bead. If this interferes with the design, such as when using a bead cap or when you want the next bead in the design to rest up tight against the large-holed bead, try using small silicone earring backs (often found on French ear wires to prevent earrings from slipping out) instead of a bicone—the silicone backs will slide inside the large hole of the bead you wish to stabilize. This also works great to keep glass focal beads from spinning on a wire pin.

—The Hole Affair

---

this project is from

Sweet Bea

17516 Minnetonka Blvd.
Minnetonka, MN 55345
(952) 473-9671
info@mysweetbeads.com
www.mysweetbeads.com

"At Sweet Beads, the creative skills are flowing and powerful," says owner Laurie Stoltenberg, who opened the shop in 2002. Laurie's philosophy calls for lots of friendly instruction. Whether you're attending a new beader's workshop, an intermediate wireworking class, or a course in more advanced beadweaving techniques, the experienced teachers are always willing to encourage a new idea. Sweet Beads also caters to children, offering kits and classes geared for young people, and the store often hosts birthday parties. Laurie has found that many customers like to sign up for private classes with their friends, combining a great social experience with learning a new skill.

"This is a place where all beaders feel comfortable letting their creativity shine," she says of her store, which features brightly colored walls and wide, comfortable worktables. A new realm of possibilities opened in 2004, when the shop began stocking yarns, hand-dyed silk cording, and other alternate fibers, in addition to oodles of beads, charms, findings, tools, and supplies. Due to overwhelming popularity, Sweet Beads began to offer classes in knitting, crochet, and bead embellishment.

"Some people may come in with a vague idea of how to start, and others come with a specific look they would like to create," Laurie says. "No matter what the starting point, they can leave with a finished beaded treasure."

Figure 1

Figure 2

Black Tie Affair

Step 1: Carefully snip the sharp point of one metal pin with the wire cutters.

Step 2: Dip one end of one pin in the glue, coating it all around the tip. Quickly insert the coated tip into one charm and lay the pin on the folded washcloth with the charm extending out over the edge of the fold. When dry, string one 2.5mm round.

Step 3: File the end of the wire smooth. Using the round-nose pliers and working on the end of the wire, make a simple loop that is large enough to fit on the pin but not larger than the flat round.

Step 4: Place the end of the pin in the wire loop and slide the wire loop up next to the bottom of the 2.5mm round.

Step 5: Holding the wire out away from the pin, string 1 flat round, one 8mm round, 1 teardrop, one 8mm round, and 1 flat round.

Step 6: Place glue on the pin with a toothpick just under the faceted bead, and string one 2.5mm round. (Figure 1.)

Step 7: Using the chain-nose pliers, begin making right-angle bends in the wire every ½" (1.3 cm), working down toward the end of the pin and around the beads. Finish by wrapping the wire around the pin just below the last bead; trim the wire close. (Figure 2.)

Step 8: Repeat Steps 1–7 three times.

Green Apple Glitz

Step 1: *Repeat Steps 1–2 above but begin by gluing on 1 green 4mm round instead of the silver 2.5mm round. String 1 lampworked bead, 1 rondelle, 1 chiclet, and one 6mm round.

Step 2: Place glue on the pin with a toothpick just under the 6mm round, and string 1 sterling silver 2.5mm round.

Step 3: Repeat Steps 1–2 three times.

Sea Foam Spirals

Leah Hanoud

This necklace is a perfect project for the intermediate to advanced beader who wants to pick up a needle and thread. The repeated loops are easy to master, the finishing is a cinch (no clasp is needed because the spiral rope is attached to a preexisting chain), and the final product is simply spectacular.

Materials
3 g sage green metallic size 11° Delicas
56 peridot AB2X 4mm Swarovski
   crystal bicones
54" (137 cm) of 6 lb test Fireline
14" (35.5 cm) of sterling silver fine-link
   Rollo chain with clasp

Tools
Size 12 English beading needle
Wire cutters

Technique
Spiral stitch

TIP Make Samples
✔ Use head pins to test samples or groupings of stones, spacers, and beads while shopping to see how they look before you commit to buying or stringing the materials.
                    —Bead Angels Bead Shop

Finished Size
18" (46 cm)

Step 1: String 8 Delicas and 1 bicone. Pass through all beads to form a circle, leave a 4–5" (10–13 cm) tail, pass through again, exiting next to the tail. Tie the tail and working thread in a square knot. (Figure 1.)

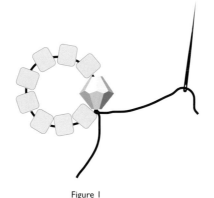

Figure 1

this project is from

Turquoise/ String Beads

**420 Quequechan St.
Fall River, MA 02723
(508) 677-1877
www.turquoise-stringbeads.com**

Twenty years ago, Nancy Valentine opened Turquoise to showcase handmade beaded accessories and Indian jewelry from the Southwest. She quickly realized that her customers wanted not only to shop, but also to learn. "Customers began asking for 'real' classes, not just the occasional demos that we'd do on the floor showing how to make popular pieces that were for sale," she says.

Nancy added String Beads to the title of the store and began stocking loose beads and other jewelry-making supplies. The shop currently has about a dozen teachers, some with national reputations, who offer a variety of classes on stringing, wireworking, beadweaving, loomwork, and more. "Our classrooms are rarely empty," she says. The staff is led by Leah Hanoud, who began working for Nancy when she was fifteen years old. Eight years later, Leah continues to be one of the driving forces behind the creation of new classes and workshops featured at the store.

Events like trunk shows, sales, and special guests ranging from lampworkers to stone cutters keep the store lively. In 2006, Nancy expanded the store again to accommodate bridal jewelry.

The Southwestern gemstones that Nancy loves shine in the roomy shop—shoppers can't miss the all-turquoise skull behind the front counter. In addition to stones including turquoise, coral, gaspeite, and sudulite, you'll find Czech and Japanese seed beads, a huge selection of crystals, and unique findings. A wide selection of tools, supplies, and reference materials are also available to spark shoppers' creativity. "I'm blessed with an artistic staff, eager to please our clientele with custom orders," Nancy says. "This is truly a beader's store."

VARIATION The silver Sea Foam Spirals Necklace is made with 2mm sterling silver seamless balls in place of the Delicas and white AB 4mm Swarovski crystal bicones in place of the peridot AB2X bicones. When working Step 5, replace the bicones with balls.

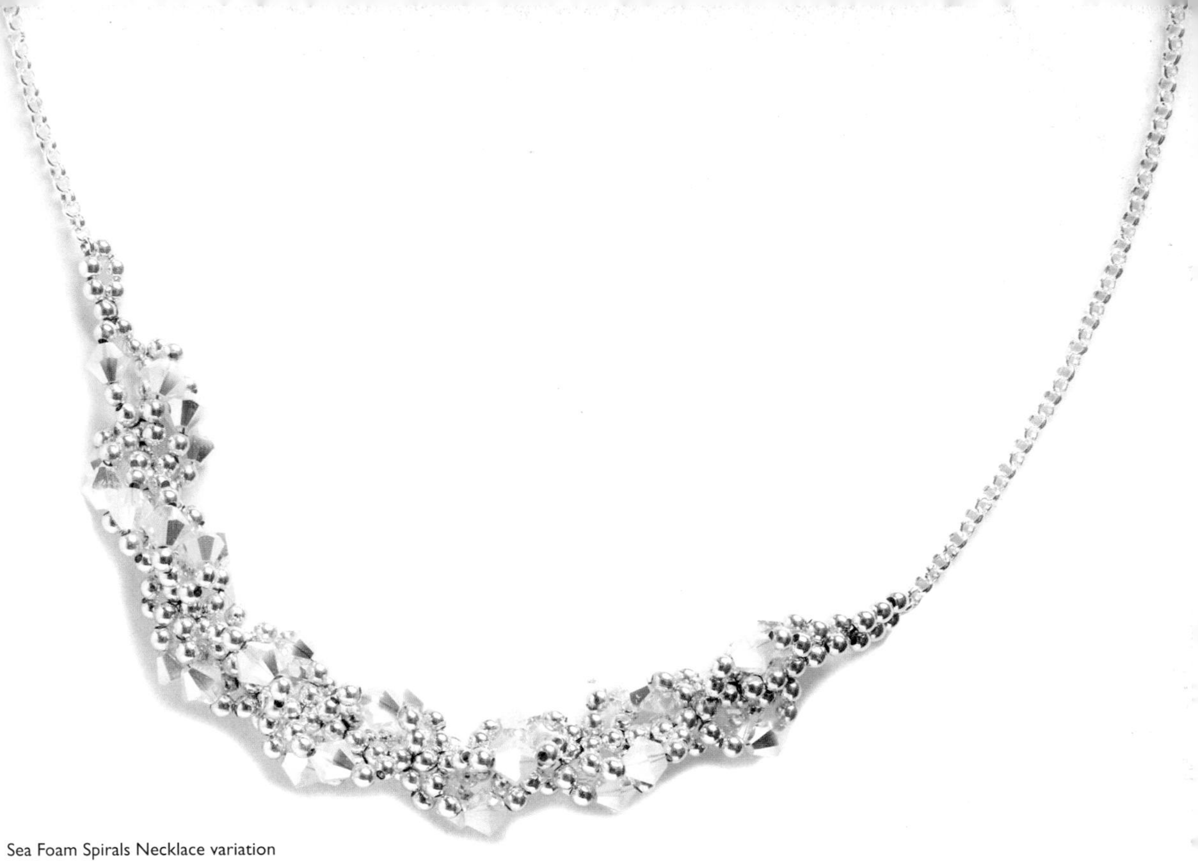

Sea Foam Spirals Necklace variation

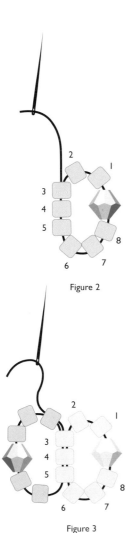

Figure 2

Figure 3

Step 2: Pass through the loop and exit between the second and third Delica. Hold the beads so that the thread is exiting out of the top of the loop. (Figure 2.)

Step 3: String 3 Delicas, 1 bicone, and 2 Delicas. Pass through the fifth, fourth, and third Delicas of the previously formed loop (the bead above the bicone always counts as the first bead) and the first strung bead of this new loop. (These last four beads passed through are the beginning of the spiral's core.) (Figure 3.) Push this new loop to the right so that it is stacked on top of the first loop and the thread is still exiting out of the top of the loop.

Step 4: Making sure to always push the new loops to the right, repeat Step 3 until the spiral measures 3¼" (8 cm).

Step 5: Cut the chain in half and string 1 bicone, 3 Delicas, pass through the last link of one of the pieces of chain, string 3 Delicas, and pass back through the bicone. Weave the thread through a loop in the spiral, tie a square knot, pass back through the loop that attaches to the chain, and tie a square knot. Pass through the core until the needle comes out of the other side.

Step 6: Repeat Step 5 to attach the other side of the spiral to the end link on the other piece of chain. Instead of passing through the core until the needle comes out of the other side, weave the thread tails into several loops and trim the thread close.

Wispy Wire Earring Stand

Arturo Rodriguez

Boca Loca Beads's master jeweler and a second-generation jeweler from Peru, Arturo isn't called the "Latino MacGyver" for nothing! He initially created the earring stands as a simple way to display accessories in the shop, but customers soon began requesting classes to learn his technique. This wire stand is simple yet elegant, requires just a few materials, and can be dressed up with crystals or elaborate lampworked beads for a bolder look. To make the Spirals and Squiggles Earrings seen with the stand, see page 48.

Materials
1 green and purple 20×62mm
 lampworked bead
22" (56 cm) of sterling silver
 16-gauge wire
1 dowel about 1" (2.5 cm) in diameter

Tools
Wire cutters
Round-nose pliers
Chain-nose pliers

Technique
Wireworking

Finished Size
4×4" (10×10 cm)

TIP Practice Makes Perfect

✔ First practice making the small and large loops with copper or brass wire—your lines will be perfectly smooth when you make the earring stand.

—Boca Loca Beads

Step 1: Find the center of the wire and bend into an S shape using the round-nose pliers (Figure 1).

Step 2: Wrap the left end of the wire counterclockwise around the dowel to create a larger loop. Repeat with the right end of the wire. The two wire ends will overlap over the center of the S. (Figure 2.)

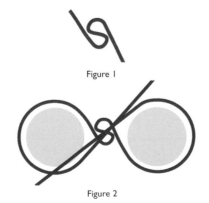

Figure 1

Figure 2

this project is from

Boca Loca Beads Inc.

872 Massachusetts Ave.
Indianapolis, IN 46204
(317) 423-2323
bocalocabeads@aol.com
www.bocalocabeadsinc.com

Boca Loca Beads opened in the summer of 1989, but owner Jari Sheese says it was truly born five years earlier on the streets of Lima, Peru. As a college student, Jari spent a year in an overseas study program in Peru, South America, where she fell in love with all aspects of Peruvian culture. She even spent six months as a street artisan, selling her jewelry and living off the meager sum she made each day. This life-changing experience molded what was to become a career as the proprietor of Boca Loca Beads.

The shop has a truly international flavor. Meaning "crazy mouth" in Spanish, Boca Loca is named after Jari's daughter, who was so talkative as a child that her family couldn't help but give her the fond nickname. The staff of Boca Loca hails from as far away as Peru and Russia and draws on more than twenty years of beading experience.

Customers can choose from a wide array of beads, materials, and tools, and learn to use them in over thirty different classes, ranging from silversmithing, bead stitching, and lampworking to wire bending with Boca Loca's "master wire bender of the universe," Arturo Rodriguez from Peru.

Jari keeps her passion for beads alive by traveling the world in search of unique and beautiful treasures, both for the shop and her personal collection. She dreams of opening a museum one day for her collection. Whether traveling in the Czech Republic to find a vintage stash of glass beads and buttons, or in a skyscraper in Kowloon, Hong Kong, marveling at the latest gemstones to hit the market, Jari says she is always thinking about her loyal customers—whom she also calls friends.

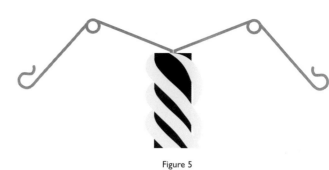

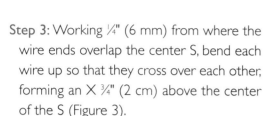

Figure 3

Figure 4

Figure 5

Step 3: Working ¼" (6 mm) from where the wire ends overlap the center S, bend each wire up so that they cross over each other, forming an X ¾" (2 cm) above the center of the S (Figure 3).

VARIATION The silver earring stand with the diamond-shaped opening is made with 22" (56 cm) of 16-gauge sterling silver wire, by omitting the lampworked bead in Step 4, twisting together the vertical wires for 1¼" (3.2 cm), separating the wires, creating a 45-degree angle in each wire to form a diamond-shaped opening, rejoining the wires, and twisting the wires together again for ½" (1.3 cm). To fill the diamond-shape opening with accent beads, wrap one end of a 6" (15 cm) piece of 22-gauge sterling silver wire around one wire of the stand near the top of the diamond-shape, string 1 blue 3mm crystal bicone, 1 clear 7×7mm crystal cube, 1 blue 3mm crystal bicone, and wrap the end of the wire of the stand near the bottom of the diamond; trim the wire close.

The copper earring stand is made with 20" (51 cm) of 16-gauge copper wire and by simply wrapping the wires only halfway around the dowel in Step 2, omitting the lampworked bead, and twisting the vertical wires for 1½" (3.8 cm) in Step 4.

Step 4: Firmly hold the wires below the X intersection with the chain-nose pliers. Using your fingers, twist the wires twice. Use both wires to string the lampworked bead.

Step 5: Looking down on the lampworked bead to ensure that wires will be aligned over the figure-eight shape of the base, use the round-nose pliers just above the bead to bend the wires down at a 45-degree

angle (Figure 4); the earrings that hang from these wires will hang directly above the loops of the figure-eight shape.

Step 7: Working 1" (2.5 cm) from the lampworked bead and using the round-nose pliers, create a downward-facing loop so that the wire exits at a 135-degree angle to the wire between the loop just formed and the lampworked bead. Bend each end up creating a shepherd's hook. (Figure 5.)

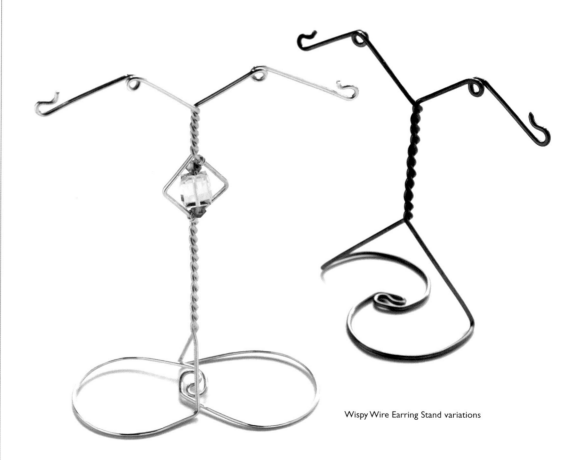

Wispy Wire Earring Stand variations

Curly Qs
● ● ● ● ● ●

Tiffany Vancil

This high-energy necklace is fun, festive, and a great project for a beginner. The twisty design is created by curling beading wire along the closed edge of a pair of scissors, the same technique to curl ribbon for a gift. The size 8° Delicas are perfect for this necklace because they are lightweight and don't weigh down the curled wire.

Materials
- 12 g amethyst size 8° Delicas
- 30 amethyst 4mm Swarovski crystal bicones
- 30 light topaz 4mm Swarovski crystal bicones
- 6 gold-filled 2×2mm crimp tubes
- 1 gold-filled lobster clasp
- 9" (23 cm) of gold-filled chain
- 42" (106.5 cm) of .014 beading wire
- 6" (15 cm) of gold-filled 22-gauge wire

Tools
- Wire cutters
- Chain-nose pliers
- Crimping pliers
- Round-nose pliers
- Scissors

Techniques
- Stringing, wireworking, crimping

Finished Size
- 19" (48 cm)

TIP Stick with Small Beads

✔ When experimenting with beads, stick to using size 8° beads or smaller; anything larger will weigh down the curl in the wire.

—Castleander Beads & Crafts

Step 1: Cut the beading wire in thirds. Using the chain-nose pliers, divide the chain into two even pieces. Set aside 1 amethyst and 1 light topaz crystal for the clasp. Begin by pulling each piece of beading wire along the edge of a closed scissors as if you are curling ribbon for a gift; make the wire very curly as the beads will weigh down the wire. Using a crimp tube, crimp one end

this project is from

Castleander Beads & Crafts

99 Lowell Rd. #5
Hudson, NH 03051
(603) 594-0048
castleander@hotmail.com
www.castleander.com

For a casual and cozy beading experience, visit Castleander Beads & Crafts, owned by mother-and-daughter team Janet Tonnesen and Tiffany Vancil. The store was originally conceived as a bead and yarn shop, reflecting Janet's knitting fixation and Tiffany's beading addiction. "The beads quickly took over," Tiffany says.

The store is truly a family affair: at least once a week Tiffany's father, Bruce, works the registers; her sister, Heather, designs bags for knitting supplies and is Castleander's graphic designer; and her husband, Buck, is the resident handyman.

Several times a week the store holds classes in various techniques, from stringing and wireworking to right-angle weave and square stitch. Castleander's website lists class information and project photographs, along with difficulty levels for each class, so students know what to expect before they enroll. For up-to-the-minute shop information, Castleander has a blog that lists regular updates about sale items, new products, and classes.

Castleander stocks a variety of beads, from all types and sizes of crystals to seed beads, semi-precious stones and pearls, findings, and more. "We have a fairly small space with a lot of beads, but everything is organized," says Tiffany. "We love to see what creations our customers come up with. We're fortunate to have a place where we love to go every day, and we want everyone who comes in to look forward to their next trip."

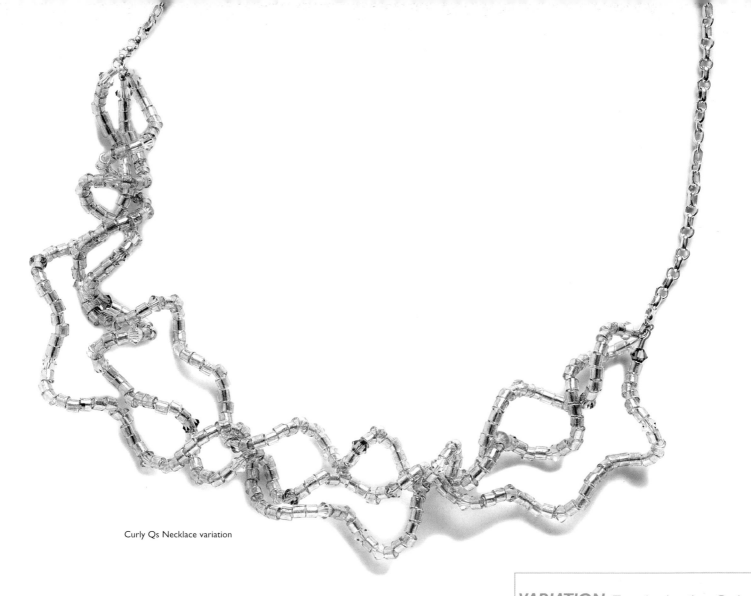

Curly Qs Necklace variation

of each piece of beading wire to one end of one piece of chain.

Step 2: Working with one beading wire, string 1 crystal, a random mix of amethyst and light topaz crystals and Delicas for 15½" (39.5 cm), 1 crystal, and 1 crimp tube. Repeat for all three strands and crimp each strand to one end of the remaining piece of chain.

Step 3: Using 3" (7.5 cm) of the 22-gauge wire and the round-nose pliers, make a wrapped loop enclosing the free end of one piece of chain. String 1 amethyst crystal and make a large wrapped loop in the end of the wire.

Step 4: Using the remaining 3" (7.5 cm) of the 22-gauge wire and the round-nose pliers, make a wrapped loop enclosing the free end of the other piece of chain. String 1 light topaz crystal. Enclosing the end of the clasp, make a wrapped loop in the end of the wire.

VARIATION To make the silver Curly Qs Necklace, follow Steps 1–4 using the following materials in place of those in the materials box: 12 g light gray AB size 8° Delicas; a mix of 46 yellow, pink, peach, light green, and lavender 4mm Swarovski crystal bicones; 6 sterling silver 2×2mm crimp tubes; 1 sterling silver lobster clasp; 9" (23 cm) of sterling silver chain; 42" (106.5 cm) of .014 beading wire; and 6" (15 cm) of sterling silver 22-gauge wire.

The Bead Shop

158 University Ave.
Palo Alto, CA 94301
(650) 328-7925
janice@beadshop.com
www.beadshop.com

When Janice Parsons opened her shop in the early 1980s, she focused on a single vision: to create the best bead shop imaginable. With a thriving Web business, www.beadshop.com, that exports to almost every country in the world, a skilled and design-savvy staff, and national media recognition, you might say The Bead Shop in Palo Alto, California, has reached that lofty objective.

"Every day we work hard to meet that goal by offering the newest and best products, design ideas, and classes in the marketplace," Parsons says. "My mission from day one has always been to share creativity and beading knowledge with our students and customers."

This shop has a distinctly modern feel: jewelry samples and hanks of stones line each wall, and bead trays hold elegant piles of sparkling stones and crystals. "Our shop is more like a design studio than a bead store," Parsons says. "Our customers gather up all kinds of goodies, from gemstones to gold, and get advice on techniques and design."

The Bead Shop offers classes ranging from knotting, stringing, lampworking, and metalsmithing to jewelry marketing. To assist the learning process, the store offers an assortment of handouts, books, magazines, DVDs, CDs, and videos. The shop's website offers downloadable instructions and helpful beading tips.

In 2004, Janice added a new dimension to the shop with the launch of Luxe Jewels, www.luxejewels.com, a direct sales company that teaches clients to host in-home jewelry-making parties.

Gems of the Earth

Janice Parsons

Inspired by a summer landscape, this project is a great way to incorporate favorite beads from your stash. Stringing together beads of all shapes and sizes that you never thought would match encourages you to explore your creativity. The special closure of this necklace, a large-holed bead with a simple suede ribbon, merges multiple strands into a single strand without unsightly knots or crimps.

> **_TIP_** Fill it Up
> ✔ Your strands do not have to be exactly the same length—for a fuller look, make the longest strand at least 1" (2.5 cm) longer than the shortest strand.
>
> —The Bead Shop

Materials
775–825 assorted clear, light to dark green, transparent gray, and white Japanese seed beads and 3–30mm semiprecious beads, freshwater pearls, crystals, and glass beads
2 green foil-lined 13mm round beads with large holes
2 clear 6mm Swarovski crystal faceted round beads
2 olivine 7×5mm Swarovski crystal faceted rondelles
16 gold-filled 1×2mm crimp tubes
2 gold-filled 2×2mm crimp tubes
2 gold-filled 3mm crimp covers
2 gold-filled 8mm soldered rings
15' (4.5 m) of gold .014 beading wire
13" (33 cm) of dark olive 8mm suede ribbon
Clear tape

Tools
Wire cutters
Crimping pliers
Needle-nose pliers

Techniques
Stringing, crimping

Finished Size
16" (40.5 cm)

Step 1: Cut eight 19" (48.5 cm) pieces of wire. Place a piece of tape 2" (5 cm) from one end of each piece of wire.

Step 2: Set aside the two 13mm beads, two 6mm crystals, and two 7×5mm crystals. String each wire with 14½–15" (35.5–38 cm) of assorted beads, using the lighter shades on the ends and darker colors in the center. Tape the ends.

Step 3: Working on one side, remove the tape from two strands and string both ends through one 1×2mm crimp tube; using the needle-nose pliers, firmly flatten the crimp bead (Figure 1). Remove the tape and string the other two ends through a second 1×2mm crimp tube and crimp. Repeat with the six remaining strands and check all strands are secure.

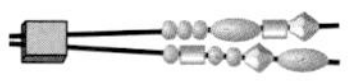

Figure 1

Step 4: Trim the excess wire ¹⁄₁₆" (2 mm) from the crimp tubes on all strands.

Step 5: Cut one 8" (20.5 cm) piece of wire and weave it between the eight strands on one side, under the crimp tubes. String both ends of the 8" (20.5 cm) piece of wire through one 13mm bead to conceal the crimp tubes (Figure 2), one 7×5mm crystal (this crystal will fit all the way or partially inside the 13mm bead to keep it firmly in place), and one 6mm crystal. Tape the wires together and set aside.

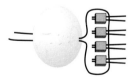

Figure 2

Step 6: Repeat Step 5 on the other side.

Step 7: Working on one side of the necklace, remove the tape, string both ends of the wire through one 2×2mm crimp tube and one ring, pass back through the crimp tube, crimp, and trim the wires close. Repeat on the other side.

Step 8: Cover crimp tubes with crimp covers.

Step 9: Thread the ribbon through the rings and tie.

Talisman Lariat and Bracelet

● ●

Cynthia Deis

Cynthia's Talisman Lariat is an ideal way to use the special charms and beads that are too powerful to leave in your bead box but never seem to find a home in any other project. The bracelet is a perfect complement, taking advantage of the silk strands left over from the lariat. Try replacing the silk cord with leather or double-sided velvet ribbon for an edgy or luscious look. The mix of beads and charms speaks to the gypsy in everyone.

Materials
15–20 assorted 6–40mm stones, charms,
   and focal beads
12–15 assorted 4–8mm Bali silver spacers
3–4 assorted Bali silver or sterling silver
   bead caps to coordinate with focal beads
2 Bali silver 3-hole 12×4mm spacer bars
12 crimp-on hook-style size 1.6 (or size
   needed to fit silk) leather ends
20 sterling silver 3" (7.5 cm) long head pins
2 Bali silver toggle clasp rings
1 Bali silver toggle clasp bar
5 sterling silver 6mm jump rings
12" (30.5 cm) of sterling silver 20-gauge wire
1 strand each of 36" (91.5 cm) long hand-dyed
   rolled silk cord in gray, dark mustard, and
   dark brown
Gum Arabic

Tools
Chain-nose pliers
Round-nose pliers
Scissors
Wire cutters

Techniques
Stringing, wireworking

Finished Size
31½" (80 cm) lariat; 7¾" (19.5 cm) bracelet

Note: Many charms used in this project are available from Green Girl Studios; (828) 298-2263; www.greengirlstudios.com.

Lariat

Step 1: Cut the gray cord to 27" (68.5 cm) long, the dark mustard cord to 25" (63.5 cm) long, and the dark brown cord to 23" (58.5 cm) long. Set aside the remaining material for the bracelet. Seal the ends of the silk cord using Gum Arabic. To aid in stringing, twist the ends to points while they dry.

Step 2: While the silk is drying, sort beads, spacers, and bead caps into six groups, based on where you want them to appear in the necklace. Pay attention to weight; try to balance out a heavy group on one end with a lighter group on the other side. Determine which beads will slide onto the silk and which will need to hang from head pins or jump rings.

this project is from

Ornamentea

509 N. West St.
Raleigh, NC 27603
(919) 834-8634
info@ornamentea.com
www.ornamentea.com

Visitors to Ornamentea may feel as if they've walked into an old-time general store—one stocked with beads, ribbons, and craft supplies instead of dry goods! The walls of this old warehouse-turned-bead shop are cleverly finished with vintage wallpaper, and beads of every sort are organized in chic antique juice glasses and displayed on an old-fashioned candy counter.

Owner Cynthia Deis credits the shop's eclectic collection of goods to her background as a designer for companies like Anthropologie and Sundance. Ornamentea stocks thousands of strands of Czech glass beads, loose glass beads, buttons, semiprecious stone beads and pearls, wire, chain, and unique findings. Other products include European and Japanese ribbons, vintage paper ephemera, stickers, polymer clay, leather, and an impressive selection of craft books in English, Japanese, and Thai.

Since opening in 1999, the store has quadrupled in size and is now home to numerous beginner and advanced classes on subjects from wireworking, stringing, and knotting to Art Clay Silver workshops. Ornamentea also offers instruction to young beaders. Shoppers are encouraged to stop by on Thursday evenings for free demonstrations of different craft techniques.

Check out the staff's online gallery for a taste of their bold creativity and the many online tutorials and tips: beginner and intermediate tutorials include step-by-step photographs and instructions. Whether you're in need of new beads, a little instruction, or just some good old-fashioned charm, stop by Ornamentea.

Step 3: When the ends of the silk are dry, run each end through a hole in one spacer bar. Select the beads from each grouping that will be added to each strand of silk and string about 2–3 beads on each strand. After the last bead is strung on each strand, run a leather end on the silk and then run the silk back through the leather end, leaving just a small amount exposed; crimp the end.

Step 4: Select one end of one strand of silk to attach a toggle ring to. Snip one end off of the hook and use the round-nose pliers to bend it inward, making a loop you can open (Figure 1). Repeat on all ends of all strands of silk.

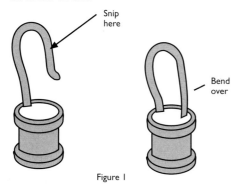

Figure 1

Step 5: Attach the toggle ring to one leather end and attach charms to the toggle ring, using jump rings, or making wrapped loops with head pins. Place other bead and spacer combinations onto head pins, make wrapped loops, and attach them to the crimp ends made in Step 3. Reserve the extra wire when you cut a head pin to use for wrapping other beads. Use additional wire as necessary.

Bracelet

Step 1: Cut each remaining strand of silk to equal the circumference of your wrist. Measure your toggle and subtract the length from your usual bracelet length. Cut the silk ½" (1.3 cm) longer than this measurement. Seal the ends of the silk cord using Gum Arabic. To aid in stringing, twist the ends to points while they dry.

Step 2: When the ends of the silk are dry, run each end through one hole in one spacer bar. Run one leather crimp end on one end of one strand of silk and then run the silk back through the crimp, leaving just a small amount exposed. Crimp the end. Repeat for all ends.

Step 3: As in Step 4 for the lariat, snip one end off of the first hook and use the round-nose pliers to bend it inward, making a loop you can open. Repeat on all ends.

Step 4: Attach one 6mm jump ring to the toggle ring and all three hooks on one end to the jump ring. Attach one 6mm jump ring to the toggle bar and the remaining three hooks to the toggle bar.

TIP Experiment with Design

✔ If you see a design you want to make but do not have the exact beads specified, do not be deterred. Substitute the colors and sizes, or approximate sizes, called for in a design with your favorite beads for a truly one-of-a-kind project.

—The Bead Tree

Twisted Fringe Tassels

Doris Weinbaum

The playful, shimmering mix of Delicas, crystals, tubular peyote stitch, and twisted fringe makes this spectacular light-reflecting accessory irresistible. Wear this lariat wrapped around your neck, hang it in a window, make just one tassel for your curtain or fan pull, or jazz up the corners of a vintage pillow.

Materials
- 7.5 g each of silver-lined chartreuse, dark fuchsia AB, and light rose AB size 11° Delicas
- 180 olivine 4mm Swarovski crystal bicones (A)
- 31 fuchsia 4mm Swarovski crystal bicones (B)
- 11 light rose 4mm Swarovski crystals bicones (C)
- 10 fuchsia 6mm Swarovski crystal bicones
- 2 olivine 8mm Swarovski crystal bicones
- 1 clear 18mm Swarovski crystal disco ball
- 2 sterling silver 2×2mm crimp tubes
- Size D beading thread in color to complement beads
- 45" (114.5 cm) of .014 beading wire

Tools
- Size 10 beading needle
- Wire cutters
- Crimping pliers

Techniques
- Stringing, tubular peyote stitch, fringe

Finished Size
- 3" (7.5 cm) tassels; 39¼" (99.5 cm) lariat

Peyote Fringe Tassel

Step 1: Working with the needle and thread, make one tube in peyote stitch in one color of your choice of Delicas that is 28 beads around and 18 rows long. To continue on with the same thread, rotate the tube so that the last row is the top.

Step 2: Embellishment loops can be made in your choice of colors and patterns; vary the pattern and colors for more interest. To make loops, *pass through the bead in the previous row (next to where your thread is coming out) and the next up bead in the same row. Pick up 3 Delicas and pass through the next up bead in the same row. Repeat from * around the entire row for a total of seven embellishment loops.

Step 3: At end of the row, work the needle down to the third row, in position to add the next loop. To do so, you will need to pass through 4 beads. (Figure 1.) *String 3 Delicas and pass through the next bead in that row. *Note:* The next bead in this row is only one bead away; be careful to follow the same row's line. Then pass through the

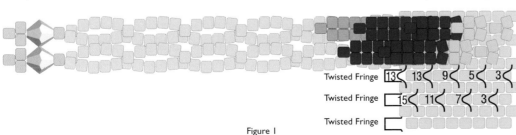

Twisted Fringe 13 13 9 5 3
Twisted Fringe 15 11 7 3
Twisted Fringe

Figure 1

this project is from
Bead in Hand

145 Harrison St.
Oak Park, IL 60304
(708) 848-1761
beadinhand@bigplanet.com
www.beadinhand.com

You won't find any signs that read "Don't handle the beads!" in Bead in Hand. According to owner Doris Weinbaum, the experience is all about touching the strands, baskets, and packages of beads to find the special treasure you've been looking for. Located in the Harrison Street Arts District in Oak Park, Illinois, this charming shop is small but cozy, with wood floors, tables, and shelves. Packed with a variety of beads, supplies, and findings, there is plenty to keep beaders occupied for hours. Head for the center table to find bins filled with pendants and stone, ceramic, glass, and metal beads. The walls are lined with semiprecious stones, pearls, glass beads, crystals, and hanks and tubes of seed beads. "You never know what you'll find," she says. "Our inventory has grown over the twelve years I've been open, and it's always changing."

Though the shop is modest in size, Doris keeps the schedule full of events, so there's never a shortage of inspiration for her customers. Beader's Night Out is a free event held the first Tuesday of every month, the perfect opportunity for women and men to chat with other beaders while working on a project. The shop regularly holds classes on a variety of seed bead techniques, wireworking, and chain making, as well as kids' birthday parties, adult parties, and trunk shows. To push her customers' creativity to the next level, Doris chooses a theme for her yearly Bead Challenge, encourages customers to submit their ideas, and then awards gift certificates to the best entries. "It is so much fun to see what different people do with an idea," she says.

bead in the previous row, next to where the thread is coming out, and the next bead in the same row (again being careful to stay on the same line). Repeat from * around the entire row for a total of seven embellishment loops.

Step 4: Repeat Step 3 seven times, adding loops to every other row and increasing the number of beads used to create the loops to 5, 7, 9, 11, 13, and 15. For the last row, string 13 beads per loop.

Step 5: To finish the top, pass through one bead in the top row. String 1 Delica, one 4mm crystal, 1 Delica, one 8mm crystal, and 9 Delicas to form a loop at the top. Go back down through the 8mm crystal, the Delica, the 4mm crystal, and the first Delica. Pass through the next bead in the top row. *String 1 Delica, pass through the next bead in the top row, string 1 Delica, one 4mm crystal, 1 Delica, go up through the 8mm crystal around the 9 Delicas in the loop, and back down through the 8mm crystal, the Delica, the 4mm crystal, and the first Delica. Pass through the next bead in the top row. Repeat from * five more times, passing through the 8mm crystal and the 9 Delicas in the loop each time. If it gets too crowded in the Delicas on the last few beads, knot the thread around the other thread above the 8mm crystal and go back through the 8mm crystal without going through the loop.

Step 6: The twisted fringe is worked in the bottom row of the peyote tube. Pass through the up bead, string 30 Delicas, 1 Delica of a different color, one 4mm olivine bicone, and 3 Delicas. Pass back through the olivine bicone and the Delica of a different color. Pull the thread so that the bicone is tight against the strung Delica.

String 30 more Delicas. With your finger and thumb close to the beads, tightly hold the thread and twist the thread until it twists back on itself. Fold the thread in half and allow the two halves to twist together. Pass through the same up bead the fringe was started on and make a small, tight knot to secure the twisted fringe. Pass through the next bead in the previous row to get to the next up bead. Attach fringe on each up bead, for a total of 14. After all fringes have been added, work all ends in and trim the threads close.

Disco Ball Tassel

Step 1: Working with the needle and thread and leaving a 6" (15 cm) thread tail, string the disco ball crystal, one 8mm crystal, and 9 Delicas.

Step 2: Pass back through the 8mm crystal to form a loop and bring the needle out between the 8mm crystal and the disco ball. String 1 Delica, 1 fuchsia 4mm bicone, and 3 Delicas. Pass back through the bicone and the first Delica, then down through the disco ball; tie a knot at the bottom with the thread tail.

Step 3: Make twisted fringe as in Step 6 above.

Step 4: Go back up through the disco ball, the 8mm crystal, and around the 9 Delicas in the loop.

Step 5: Repeat Steps 2–4 until you have six 4mm fuchsia bicones in between the 8mm crystal and the disco ball. Continue to make fringe in the same manner, but go down through the 8mm crystal and the disco ball without adding any beads in between. You will be going through the disco ball, the 8mm crystal, and the 9 Delicas in the loop each time. (We made a total of 9 fringes

with 4mm olivine bicones used for the tip of five fringes and 4mm fuchsia bicones for the tip of four fringes.) If it gets too crowded in the Delicas on the last few beads, knot the thread around the other threads above the 8mm crystal and go back through the 8mm crystal without going through the loop.

Lariat

Step 1: Working with the beading wire, string 1 crimp tube and 9 Delicas. String this through the loop on the Peyote Fringe Tassel. Pass back through the crimp tube and crimp, forming a new loop interlocked with the tassel; trim the wire tail close.

Step 2: String 1 Delica to start and 1 Delica between each of the following: 7A, 1B, 1C, 1B, 7A, and one 6mm crystal.

Step 3: Repeat Step 2 nine times.

Step 4: String 1 Delica and then 1 Delica between each of the following: 7A, 1B, 1C, 1B, and 7A.

Step 5: String 1 Delica, the second crimp bead, and 9 Delicas. String this through the loop on the Disco Ball Tassel. Pass back through the crimp tube and crimp, forming a new loop interlocked with the tassel; trim the wire tail close.

TIP Choose Wisely

✔ Choosing beads can be the most difficult part of starting a project. A rule of thumb: if the beads look great in a pile in your hand, they will be great in your finished project. You can take all of the fun out of a project by thinking about it too much.

—Bead Culture

362 Ludlow Ave.
Cincinnati, OH 45220
(513) 861-9626
orders@sakisilver.com
www.sakisilver.com

Saki Silver may have a home in Cincinnati, Ohio, but the company's true roots lie thousands of miles away on a beach in Bangkok, Thailand. Owners Liz and Sak Chumtong met in Thailand, where they started their business of selling their beaded art on the beach. After laying the groundwork for a company that manufacturers silver findings and beads, the couple moved to the United States, settled down in Cincinnati, and opened the Saki Silver showroom.

Saki Silver has flourished in recent years, in part due to a company philosophy of supporting family, friends, and the creative spirit. While attending tradeshows and raising two children, Liz and Sak create original designs for their store and manage a busy mail-order catalog. They still own a wholesale company in Bangkok that pays its employees well, treats them like family, and offers educational opportunities. The couple spends significant time in Thailand each year, living and working with their silversmiths in a creative environment. "We enjoy supporting the native arts of Thailand, and to be able to do business with friends and family," Liz says. "They put their heart and soul into the work, and it shows."

Though the shop is best known for its high-quality toggle clasps, available in texturized and geometric designs, Saki Silver also offers a wide array of gemstones, beads, pendants, and finished jewelry. To add even more depth to her creative repertoire, Liz is training to become a certified gemologist in 2006, hoping to add stonework to the offerings of Saki Silver. "Our goal is to be as unique as possible," Liz says. "We offer unique designs to our customers, without sacrificing the quality or integrity of our products or company."

Wild, Wild Bolo

● ● ● ● ● ● ● ● ● ● ●

Amy Boehm

This bolo, designed by Saki Silver shop manager Amy, demonstrates a distinctive way to use four-strand and triangle spacer beads. The combination of onyx, turquoise, and silver creates a bolo with feminine flair. A matching silver toggle completes the look.

Materials
4 onyx 8×14mm faceted teardrops
333 turquoise 4mm faceted rondelles
52 sterling silver 2mm faceted beads
  (unneeded if spacers are same front and back)
2 sterling silver 4mm balls
4 sterling silver 4-hole 5×19mm spacer bars
2 sterling silver two-to-one hole 13×14mm triangle spacer beads
1 sterling silver toggle clasp
6 sterling silver 2×2mm crimp tubes
52" (132 cm) of .014 beading wire

Tools
Wire cutters
Crimping pliers

Techniques
Stringing, crimping

Finished Size
14" (35.5 cm)

Step 1: Cut the wire into four 13" (33 cm) long strands, string 1 crimp tube through two strands of wire, string 1 side of the clasp, and pass both wires back through the crimp tube. Crimp and trim the wires close. String 1 silver ball through both strands of wire. Repeat this step on the other side of the clasp.

Step 2: To hide the wire on the back of the triangle spacer, bring both strands of wire through the first loop of the triangle spacer (if working with spacers that are the same on the front and the back, string the spacer and skip to Step 3). String each strand with four 2mm beads and bring each strand through one of the loops at the bottom of the triangle. String one 2mm faceted silver bead on each strand. (Figure 1.) Repeat this step on the other side of the clasp.

Figure 1

Step 3: String each of the four strands with 7½" (19 cm) of 4mm turquoise.

Step 4: Repeat Steps 1–3 on the other side of the clasp.

Step 5: String one 2mm bead, 1 spacer bar facedown, one 2mm bead, and 1 turquoise bead on each of the four strands, making sure the triangle spacers are also facedown and ensuring that the wires are not twisted so that they enter the appropriate holes of the spacer.

Step 6: Repeat Step 5 three times (Figure 2).

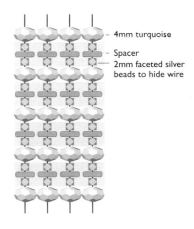

- 4mm turquoise
- Spacer
- 2mm faceted silver beads to hide wire

Figure 2

Step 7: String 1½" (3.8 cm) of turquoise on the two outside strands, 2½" (6.5 cm) on one of the inside strands, and 3" (7.5 cm) on the last inside strand.

Step 8: String 1 teardrop on each strand.

Step 9: String 1 crimp tube at the end of each strand, crimp, and trim the wires close.

Kiwi Serpentine

●●●●●●●●●●●

Donna Nickson

A beginning wireworker will feel confident making this lively bracelet. Although Donna typically works in seed beads, she put her basic wire-working knowledge to work in this project. Add a little extra length and a few beads, and the piece easily becomes a necklace for any occasion.

Materials
  112 emerald gold luster size 11° Delicas
  16 green 3mm freshwater pearls
  7 green 4mm freshwater pearls
  7 green 15mm square mother-of-pearl dyed shell
  3 copper 5mm jump rings
  1 copper toggle clasp
  56" (142 cm) of copper 26-gauge wire

Tools
  Flat-nose pliers
  Small round-nose pliers
  Wire cutters

Technique
  Wireworking

Finished Size
  7¾" (19.5 cm)

Step 1: String 1 shell on a 3¼" (8.5 cm) piece of wire, leaving a 1" (2.5 cm) tail on the left side of the shell. Using this 1" (2.5 cm) of wire, make a wrapped loop. Trim the excess wire.

TIPS

Know the Gauge of Your Wire

✔ To keep track of the wire sizes in your stash, cut 3" (7.5 cm) pieces of wire in gauges 18 to 26 and securely wrap one end of each wire to a key ring. Keep the key ring in your toolbox and use as a quick reference when determining which wire will fit through the beads you have chosen.

—Beadissimo

Be Nice to Your Tools

✔ Always use the right tool for the job. For example, don't cut wire with nippers or use scissors on memory wire. Treat your tools right to prolong their life.

—Ornamentea

---

this project is from

Ambrosia Bead Company

**5110 Tieton Dr., Ste. 230
Yakima, WA 98908
(509) 972-3750
beads@ambrosiabeadcompany.com
www.ambrosiabeadcompany.com**

Debbie Hunter had no problem naming her fledgling bead shop when it opened in 2003. Ambrosia, meaning "food of the gods," was the perfect moniker for the store she envisioned.

Debbie knew she was on to something when the shop outgrew its 375-square-foot cozy space within five months. Following two more rapid expansions, Ambrosia Bead Company now resides in a two-level 2,100-square-foot space at the front of a shopping mall.

The shop retains the ambience of the first building it occupied, a nineteenth-century fruit warehouse. The current shop's hardwood planking, rough timbers, and brick are toned down with soothing neutral paints, letting the colorful beads catch the customer's eye. "We pay particular attention to store layout and lighting," Debbie says. "Every single display has been laid out in the same color scheme, from clear to black. That makes it easy to find what you're looking for, and it really draws the eye, too."

Ambrosia prides itself on having something for everyone. The store offers a wide selection of stones, pearls, silver, vintage, Greek, African, and crystal beads, and, of course, a great selection of seed beads. Classes include beginning lampwork, wireworking, Precious Metal Clay, and more, to spark each beader's individual interest. "Everyone likes to feel special and important," Debbie says. "We work hard to make sure that happens!"

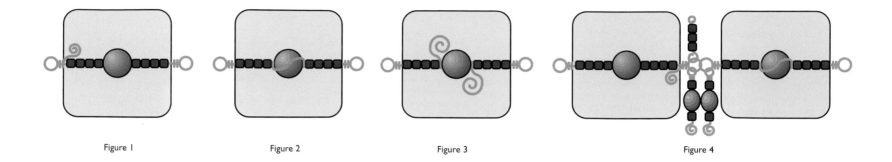

Figure 1 Figure 2 Figure 3 Figure 4

Step 2: Make a second wrapped loop on the other end of the shell, being sure to pull the wire tight. Bend the remaining wire up across the shell, and string 4 Delicas, one 4mm pearl, and 4 Delicas back toward the first loop. Twist the wire twice around the base of the first loop and bring up onto the shell. Using round-nose pliers, make a spiral in the remaining wire and press flat to the shell. (Figure 1.) Rotate the shell 180 degrees.

Step 3: When making the first wrapped loop for the second shell, link the wire in the last wrapped loop on the previous shell before wrapping. String 1 shell, make a wrapped loop, and string the beads in the same pattern established in Step 2. Do not make a spiral at the edge of the shell with the excess wire; instead, wrap the wire around the first loop and trim the wire close. Cut a 1" (2.5 cm) piece of wire. Wrap one end of this piece around the wire that crosses the shell between the fourth Delica and the pearl. Cross the wire over the top of the pearl and wrap it around the wire that crosses the shell on the other side of the

pearl, between the pearl and the fifth Delica. Trim the wire close. (Figure 2.)

Step 4: Repeat Steps 1–2 for the third shell except rotate the shell 180 degrees before making the second wrapped loop; when making the second wrapped loop, link the wire into the last wrapped loop on the previous shell before wrapping. Do not rotate the shell 180 degrees a second time.

Step 5: When making the fourth wrapped loop for the second shell, link the wire in the last wrapped loop on the previous shell before wrapping. String 1 shell, make a wrapped loop, and string the beads in the same pattern established in Step 2. Do not make a spiral at the edge of the shell with the excess wire; instead, wrap the wire around the first loop and trim the wire close. Cut a 1" (2.5 cm) piece of wire and make a spiral in one end. Slide the spiral under the wire that crosses the shell and between the fourth Delica and the pearl. Bend the wire over the wire that crosses the shell around one side of the pearl and then bend it over the wire that crosses the shell and between the pearl and fifth Delica.

Make a spiral in the end and press the spiral to the shell. (Figure 3.)

Step 6: Repeat Step 4 for the fifth shell but do not rotate 180 degrees.

Step 7: Repeat Step 3 for the sixth shell.

Step 8: Repeat Step 6 for the seventh shell.

Step 9: To add drops to the loops between the first and second shells, cut a 1½" (3.8 cm) piece of copper wire and make a small tight spiral. String 1 Delica, one 3mm pearl, 1 Delica, begin making a wrapped loop on one end, slip the end through one of the joining loops, and finish the wrapped loop. Repeat in the remaining joining loop. Connect a third drop to one of the joining loops in the same manner but using a 1" (2.5 cm) piece of wire, 3 Delicas, and a simple loop to secure the end. (Figure 4.)

Step 10: Repeat Step 9 to continue adding three drops between each shell and at the end of the first and last shell.

Step 11: Attach one jump ring to the first wrapped loop and the end of the clasp. Attach one jump ring to the last wrapped loop, add another jump ring, and join to the other half of the clasp.

Koi Lagoon Mosaic

Sarah Brownfield

Once you've mastered cutting beads with a glass nipper, this dynamic tray is simple to create from glass beads, glue, grout, and a large picture frame. Make a fun and functional tray for serving guests at your next party, enjoying breakfast in bed, or snacking in front of the television after a long day at work. Try your own design, or write a child's name in beads for a bedroom sign—the options are endless.

Materials
Assorted blue, green, red, pink, black, and white Japanese seed beads and 3–50mm pressed-glass, semiprecious beads, glass pearls, crystals, cloisonné goldfish, and lampworked beads, enough beads to cover about ⅔ of the inside of the frame
20 g green AB size 6° seed beads
24 green/aqua 8mm cathedral window beads
60 green/aqua 10–15mm leaf beads
4 crystal 1¼" (33mm) faceted glass drawer pulls with threaded shafts
32 silver 2×2mm crimp tubes
Size D beading thread in any color
4' (1.2 m) of .019 beading wire
14' (4.3 m) of green 20-gauge craft wire
35' (10.7 m) of silver 26-gauge craft wire
4 metal ½" (1.3 cm) long screws
4 metal ½" (1.3 cm) long eye screws
1 wood picture frame 17×20¾" (43×52.5 cm) with 11½×15½" (29×39.5 cm) opening
1 piece of ¼" (6 mm) thick 13¼×17½" (33.5×44.5 cm) plywood
Spackling paste
Wood priming paint
Sanded grout, in the colors of your choice
Grout sealer
Acrylic paint, in the colors of your choice
Acrylic sealer, clear
Ultimate Glue
Wood glue
Newspaper

Tools
Size 10 beading needle
Wire cutters
Crimping pliers
Glass nippers
3 paintbrushes, one ½" (1.3 cm) wide and two 3" (7.5 cm) wide
Spoon

Technique
Stringing

Finished Size
17×20¾×5" (43×52.5×12.5 cm)

Note: Materials, excluding beads, are available at stained glass and hardware stores or from online resources.

TIP Variety is Key
✔ The greater the variety bead shapes and colors used in this project, the better. Bright, iridescent-colored beads make the most interesting and vibrant mosaics.
—Third Eye Beads & Gift Gallery

---

this project is from
Third Eye Beads & Gift Gallery

434 N. El Camino Real
San Clemente, CA 92672
(949) 366-0219

At Third Eye Beads & Gift Gallery in San Clemente, California, the clientele is just as diverse as the merchandise. Owner JoAnn Sandidge's open, airy store features beads, findings, finished jewelry, body jewelry, blown glass, seashells, bamboo curtains, and other novelties. Customers include local surfers and environmentalists as well as the tourists who flock to this small beach town. "We get a wide range of customers, from little kids to grannies, and people seem to love us," says JoAnn, who opened the shop in 1997.

Although Third Eye Beads carries seed beads and beading supplies, the emphasis is on its collection of gemstones and sterling silver beads and findings. Classes are taught at a large worktable called the "bead bar," in subjects from basic beading and wireworking to Precious Metal Clay. Much of the shop's finished jewelry is created by JoAnn and shop manager Sarah Brownfield, who also teaches many of the workshops.

JoAnn also owns Capo Jo, a company that produces a line of jewelry and accessories that incorporate leather and metal. Capo Jo's presence in the wholesale jewelry market keeps JoAnn current on trends, new products, and the newest emerging styles, which in turn helps her stock the most innovative supplies.

JoAnn's favorite part of Third Eye Beads is simply helping beaders harness their creative energy. "I love owning a bead shop. I'm just amazed at how creativity is such a human need, and we love helping people realize just how creative they can be. It's very empowering," JoAnn says. "People often think they can't do it, but it's so simple."

Step 1: *Building the tray.* If necessary, remove all glass and backing material from the picture frame. Run a line of wood glue on the backside of the frame along the opening, center the plywood over the back of the frame, and press in place, wiping away any excess glue. Place one ½" (1.3 cm) long screw on each side of the plywood, ¼" (6 mm) from the edge, driving through the plywood and the inside edge of the frame. After the glue is dry, use the spackling paste to fill in any gaps between the frame and plywood. Allow spackle to dry and using a 3" (7.5 cm) wide paintbrush, coat all surfaces with the wood priming paint. Allow to dry thoroughly.

Step 2: *Transferring the pattern.* Enlarge the pattern (Figure 1) by 320 percent. Working with the frame faceup, transfer the design to the plywood: tape the pattern backward in a bright window, trace the pattern lines on the backside of the paper, lay the paper face up on the plywood, and draw over the right side of the pattern, causing the pencil lines from the backside to transfer on to the primer. If necessary, touch up the lines on the plywood by tracing them with the pencil.

Step 3: *Mosaic.* Starting with the outlines of the design in an area 6" (15 cm) square or smaller and using the assorted beads listed in the materials list (set aside all other beads), apply beads to the tray: string the thread with assorted 3–4mm beads, outline the design with Ultimate Glue, and press the strung beads into the glue outline.

Step 4: Once all of the shapes have been outlined, begin to fill in the background with larger sized glass beads (8–12mm): estimate the amount of beads needed to cover each larger area by placing loose beads in the area to be filled until about two-thirds of the area is covered. Remove the beads and begin cutting them in half with glass nippers: hold each bead straight up and down vertically (with the glass nipper blade wheels directly over the middle of the bead and the bead holes on top and bottom), and squeeze the nippers until the bead snaps in half. *Note:* You may find it helpful to hold the bead with one hand and cut with the other, without letting go of the bead. Be aware of eye safety by wearing safety glasses and/or nipping the beads inside a paper bag or under a towel. Cover the area to be filled with a generous coat of Ultimate Glue and arrange the halved beads as desired. Repeat until all areas have been filled. Allow the glue to dry for at least twenty-four hours.

Step 5: Mix the colored grout of your choice according to manufacturer's directions and, working in small sections, spoon small amounts between the beads to cover the backing and wire; do not use so much grout that it covers the beads. Allow the grout to set and dry for at least twenty-four hours.

Step 6: Seal the beads with a thin coat of grout sealer.

Step 7: Cover the mosaic with newspaper and using the acrylic paint and ½" (1.3 cm) wide paintbrush, paint the frame as desired. Once dry, seal the paint with acrylic sealer, using a 3" (7.5 cm) wide paintbrush.

Step 8: *Embellishing the tray.* Insert an eye screw in each corner of the frame, about 1" (2.5 cm) away from the mosaic. Anchoring the 20-gauge wire by wrapping the ends

Figure 1

around the eye screws, string assorted beads around the inside of the frame.

Step 9: To create fringe for the corners of the tray, cut four 6" (15 cm) pieces of beading wire. Crimp a crimp tube on one end of a piece of the beading wire. String 1 leaf bead, 26 size 6°s, 1 leaf bead and 1 crimp tube. Crimp the crimp tube, and trim the wire close. Repeat for all four wire pieces. Cut one 2½" (6.5 cm) piece of 20-gauge green craft wire and make a small wrapped loop in one end, enclosing one of the corner eye hooks. String 3 large assorted beads on the wire, end with a wrapped loop that

wraps around the middle of the four wires strung with leaf beads, and trim the wire close. Repeat this Step for the other three corners of the frame.

Step 10: *Feet.* Cut two 3" (7.5 cm) pieces of 20-gauge green craft wire. *String 1 size 6° and 1 leaf bead; repeat from * six times. Twist the wire ends together 2–3 times to form a circle and trim the wires close. *String 1 size 6° and 1 green/aqua cathedral bead; repeat from * five times and set aside. Twist the wire ends together 2–3 times to from a circle and trim the wires close. String one of the rings with leaf beads

onto the shaft of one drawer pull. Cut one 12" (30 cm) piece of 20-gauge green craft wire, wrap the end of the wire around the shaft of the drawer pull two times, and string the wire with size 6°s, leaving about 2½" (6.5 cm) of the wire unbeaded. Wrap the beaded wire up the shaft of the drawer pull and continue to wrap the unbeaded end of the wire around the shaft. Slide the ring with cathedral beads on the end of the drawer pull shaft to cover the unbeaded wire. Screw the drawer pull into the corner of the bottom of the frame.

Step 11: Repeat Step 10 for three more feet.

this project is from

Bluewater Beads Inc.

Online only
(615) 565-4945
www.bluewaterbeads.com

When Jan Mrachek settled her bead shop into a cozy little house on Tegarden Road in Gulfport, Mississippi, she never dreamed that the deep blue waters that inspired her shop's name would be the same force to change her business forever.

In a bittersweet stroke of luck, Jan was out of state in August 2005 when Hurricane Katrina swept through Gulfport and left a path of destruction in its wake. As the hurricane hit, Jan could only watch the storm and its aftermath on television. She spent several weeks mourning the loss of her shop, only to be dumbfounded by what she found at Bluewater Beads a month later.

"It was like going into the twilight zone," Jan says. "It was just unbelievable. Other houses on the street were completely wiped out, but my building was still standing." The interior of the shop looked no different than it had the night before the storm hit, with one exception: many dishes of beads had been moved from one end of the shop to the other without even jostling their contents. Jan spent five days recovering beads and materials from the house, which had withstood wind and eighteen inches (45.5 cm) of churning water.

Since Bluewater Beads could not reopen in the devastated area, Jan now focuses on her online shop. And the shop name? She insisted it will always be called Bluewater Beads, no matter what happens. Jan is thankful for the guidance and support of Beth Kraft, owner of Nordic Gypsy Beads and Jewelry in Rochester, Minnesota, since the opening of the original Bluewater Beads shop and especially for her support during the challenging times brought by Hurricane Katrina.

Spirals and Squiggles Earrings

Jan Mrachek

Jan loves making these fun earrings to practice her wireworking skills. Suitable for beaders of all levels, this project is easy to customize for any outfit. Learn the basic wire shaping methods used here and let your imagination run wild.

Materials for the Spiral Earrings
  2 purple 4×4×13mm rectangles
  2 red Czech glass 12×12mm flat triangles
  2 violet opal 4mm Swarovski crystal bicones
  2 pink shell 13mm disks
  2 pink 4mm glass pearls
  2 Bali silver 6×3mm beads
  2 Bali silver 4×1mm spacers
  24" (61 cm) each of sterling silver
    20-, 22-, and 24-gauge dead-soft wire
  3 pairs of assorted sterling silver
    French ear wires

Materials for the Squiggle Earrings
  4 blue zircon 4mm Swarovski crystal bicones
  2 turquoise stone 5×2mm beads
  2 dark abalone shell 10×20mm oval beads
  4 star-shaped Bali silver 5×1mm spacers
  24" (61 cm) of sterling silver 20-gauge
    dead-soft wire
  2 pairs of assorted sterling silver
    French ear wires

Tools
  Chain-nose pliers
  Round-nose pliers
  Wire cutter
  Chasing hammer

Technique
  Wireworking

Finished Size
  Spirals Earrings each about 1¼" (3.2 cm);
    Squiggles Earrings each about 1½" (3.8 cm)

Spiral Earrings

Step 1: *Basic spiral.* Use the basic information presented here when working the Purple Spiral and Pink Spiral Earrings. Using the round-nose pliers, make a hook on one end of a 3" (7.5 cm) piece of wire (Figure 1). With the chain-nose pliers, close the hook (Figure 2). Hold the loop in the back of the chain-nose pliers so that the long end of the wire extends away from the tip of the pliers (Figure 3). Using your hand, push the wire back toward the handle of the pliers to make a spiral, opening up the chain-nose and repositioning the wire several times to complete the spiral. You can make the spiral tight (Figure 4) or loose (Figure 5) depending on how close you push the wire. *Note:* If you are using 24-gauge wire for freshwater pearls, semiprecious stones, or other beads with small holes, hammer the spiral to give it more stability.

Figure 1   Figure 2

Figure 3

Figure 4   Figure 5

Step 2: *Purple Spiral Earrings.* Cut two 3" (7.5 cm) pieces of 22- or 24-gauge wire (depending on the size of the holes in your beads). Referring to Step 1, make a small tight spiral at one end of one piece of wire. String 1 rectangle, 1 spacer, 1 crystal, and make a wrapped loop on each wire. Slide the wrapped loop on an ear wire. Repeat for a second earring.

Step 3: *Pink Spiral Earrings.* Cut two 3" (7.5 cm) pieces of 22- or 20-gauge wire (depending on the size of the holes in your beads). Referring to Step 1, make a loose spiral at one end of one piece of wire. String 1 pink bead, press the spiral flat against the pink bead and string 1 Bali bead and 1 pearl. Make a wrapped loop in the other end of the wire and slide the loop on an ear wire. (Figure 6.) Repeat for a second earring.

Step 4: *Red Spiral Earrings.* Cut two 3" (7.5 cm) pieces of 22- or 20-gauge wire (depending on the size of the holes in your beads). Referring to Step 1, make a loose spiral at one end of one piece. String 1 red bead and press the spiral flat against the bead. Make a simple loop in the other end of the wire, bend the wire over the top of the bead so that the loop is in the center of the bead. (Figure 7.) Slide the loop on an ear wire. Repeat for a second earring.

Figure 6

Figure 7

Squiggle Earrings

Step 1: *Basic squiggle.* Use the basic information presented here when working the Emerald and Oval Squiggle Earrings. Holding two wires together so that they will match, wrap them around the round-nose pliers close to the tips of the pliers (Figure 8). Reposition the pliers and wrap the wires around the tips in the opposite direction to begin making the squiggle shape (Figure 9). After you have made the desired number of squiggles, turn the tip so it is straight (Figure 10).

Step 2: *Emerald Squiggle Earrings.* Cut two 3" (7.5 cm) pieces of 20-gauge wire. Referring to Step 1, make three squiggles and hammer the tip of the squiggle on each piece flat (Figure 11). Using the chain-nose pliers, make a right angle bend in the center of the last squiggle on each piece (Figure 12). String 1 blue zircon crystal, 1 spacer, 1 turquoise bead, 1 spacer, and 1 blue zircon crystal on each wire. Make a simple loop in the other ends of the wires and slide each loop on an ear wire.

Step 3: *Oval Squiggle Earrings.* Cut two 3" (7.5 cm) pieces of 20-gauge. Referring to Step 1, make 2–3 squiggles in the wire, depending on the exact size of your oval bead. Flatten the squiggles by hammering. String 1 oval bead on each wire, leaving enough room before the squiggle so that the squiggle will rest flat against the surface of the oval when it is bent up against the oval. Press the squiggles flat on the ovals. (Figure 13.) Make a simple loop in the other ends of the wires and slide each loop on an ear wire.

Figure 8

Figure 9

Figure 10

Figure 11

Figure 12

Figure 13

Patterned Peyote Rings Bracelet

Karina Kimpell

Since each link of this simple peyote-stitch project is only four beads wide, you'll be wearing your three-dimensional, playful bracelet after just three hours of work. Or add extra links to make a choker or draping necklace. Feel free to deviate from the patterns provided—there are no rules when it comes to color. The smart doorknocker clasp makes for effortless finishing.

Materials
2 g each of pink, lavender, orange, light green, cream, light teal, and matte royal blue size 11° silver-lined Delicas
5 g black size 11° matte opaque Delicas
1 sterling silver doorknocker clasp
Size D beading thread in color to complement beads
Beeswax

Tools
Size 10 beading needle

Technique
Peyote stitch

Finished Size
7½" (19 cm)

TIP Avoid Using Glue and Knots
✔ To avoid using glue or knots when finishing a thread, weave the needle through the holes of the beads several times until they become nearly full with thread—the resulting tension will hold the work together and keep the tail in place.

—Bead Culture

Step 1: Lightly wax 6' (2 m) of doubled thread and thread the needle, leaving an 8" (20.5 cm) tail. Following the pattern in Figure 1, work flat peyote stitch 4 beads wide by 60 rows.

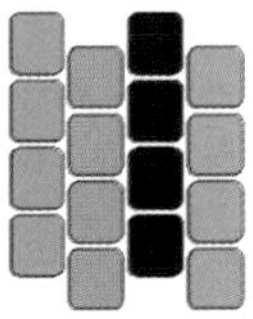

Figure 1

this project is from

Bead Culture

180 West Michigan Ave.
Jackson, MI 49201
(517) 841-9173
www.beadculture.com

At Bead Culture, owner Karina Kimpell wants every beader to focus on being imaginative and true to herself. "We create an environment where every person can feel inspired and encouraged," she says. "We do all we can to show our customers that beading and jewelry making is much more than a hobby. It's social connection, a creative release, and an escape from the everyday."

Classes are the backbone of Bead Culture. Students can sign up for instruction in basic off-loom stitches, wireworking, chain making, and other jewelry-making techniques almost every night of the week. If you don't have time to drop in on a class, visit the shop's website for free project instructions or to purchase a kit.

Karina's background in computer software composition, technical support, and graphic design help her create patterns and project instructions that are consistent and easy to read. She says it's important that Bead Culture offers projects that beaders are proud to wear, in sync with current fashion trends, and quick to complete. She believes new students are much more capable than they give themselves credit for, and her knowledgeable and encouraging staff strives to create a relaxing environment.

"Bead Culture is a safe haven to escape the stress of the everyday, explore new creative avenues, and simply hang out," Karina says. "Of course there are beads here, too, and that doesn't hurt."

Step 2: Join the last row to your first by zipping the edges together: needle through the first up bead of the first row, then the first up bead of the last row, the second up bead of the first row, and the second up bead of the last row (Figure 2). Weave the tail thread and the beginning thread through several beads to secure the link; trim the thread close.

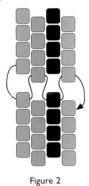

Figure 2

Step 3: Repeat Steps 1–2, enclosing the previous link before zipping the current link closed to make 17 total links, following the charts in Figures 1 and 3–18. Alternate the number of rows in each link, 60 in one link, 40 in the next. Or, adjust the number of rows in your links to any even number to make your bracelet the desired length.

Step 4: Thread the first and last link through the doorknocker clasp.

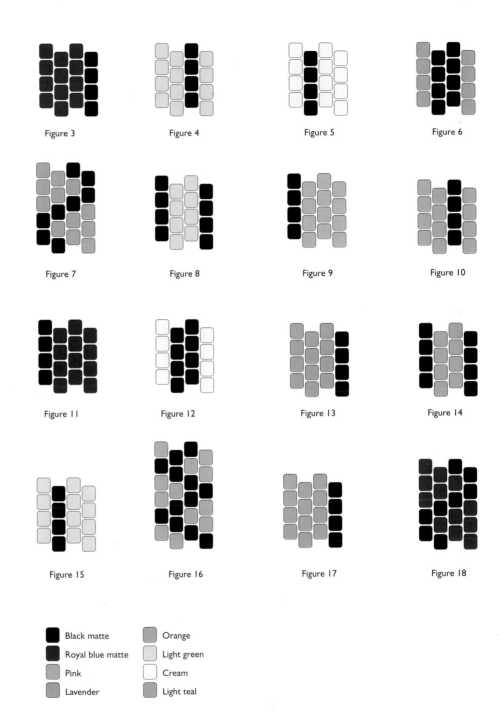

Figure 3 Figure 4 Figure 5 Figure 6

Figure 7 Figure 8 Figure 9 Figure 10

Figure 11 Figure 12 Figure 13 Figure 14

Figure 15 Figure 16 Figure 17 Figure 18

- ■ Black matte
- ■ Royal blue matte
- ■ Pink
- ■ Lavender
- ■ Orange
- □ Light green
- □ Cream
- ■ Light teal

Optical Illusion Cuff

Jeanette Shanigan

Jeanette used two-drop peyote to create this unique accessory. This inventive bracelet looks like one piece, but it's actually worked as two separate pieces that are woven together later. Make more than one of each piece in different colors and interchange them to easily match your wardrobe on any given day.

Materials
30 g each of matte green and teal AB
  size 11° Japanese seed beads
20 each of matte green and teal AB
  size 8° Japanese seed beads
2 glass 10mm round or barrel accent
  beads in colors to complement beads
1 tension bead
Size D beading thread in color
  to complement beads

Tools
Size 12 beading needle

Techniques
Two-drop peyote stitch, tension bead

Finished Size
7½" (19 cm)

Step 1: *Notes:* When referring to the Figures, the new beads added in each step are outlined in red. Work Steps 1–16 using the same color of size 11°s.

Step 2: Cut a 36" (91.5 cm) piece of thread. Leaving a 12" (30.5 cm) tail, string a tension bead. String 14 size 11°s. Pass back through the ninth and tenth beads (Figure 1a); pull taut. Work two-drop peyote with size 11°s to the end of the row for a total of two stitches (Figure 1b).

Step 3: Repeat another row of two-drop peyote with size 11°s for a total of three stitches (Figure 2).

TIP Alter the Length
✔ To make a shorter bracelet, work a total of eight points on one side and nine points on the other in Step 15; for a longer length work a total of ten points on one side and eleven points on the other. When customizing the bracelet even further, simply make sure that one side has an even number of points and the other an odd number of points.

—Alaska Bead Company

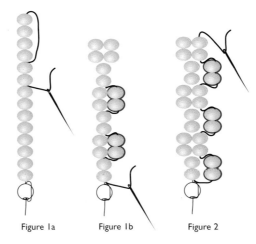

Figure 1a   Figure 1b   Figure 2

---

this project is from
Alaska Bead Company

2217 E. Tudor Rd., Ste. 7
Anchorage, AK 99507
(907) 563-2323
orders@alaskabead.com

Why does Alaska Bead Company (ABC) honor itself on being "the beader's bead store"? Judge for yourself! ABC offers a new selection of beads that is rolled out every Sunday, an array of trunk shows, original beadwork challenges to keep customers on their toes, and more than seventy-five classes taught by more than twenty teachers and celebrity guest instructors (including Diane Fitzgerald, NanC Meinhardt, Cynthia Rutledge, and Jeannette Cook).

ABC got its start more than twelve years ago when owners Mark and Jonisue Minor moved from the California Bay Area to Eagle River, Alaska, to pursue a more serene lifestyle. They purchased a small bead store that was going out of business and quickly set about learning the ropes. After just one year, they hired a manager, Linda Meyers, who began teaching and eventually amassed a repertoire of more than fifty beading and wireworking classes. Their success continued, and in 2002 the shop doubled its size to 4,000 square feet and implemented a computer system to track inventory.

Every four months, ABC offers a new schedule of classes that cover the basics of beading, bead embroidery, off-loom beadweaving, wirework, polymer clay, bead crochet, loomwork, and other techniques. They carry a full selection of beads including Japanese and Czech seed beads, Delicas, Swarovski crystals, Czech pressed and fire-polished beads, semi precious gemstones, as well as wire and findings. "Customers shouldn't have to go to several stores to find everything they need for one project," Jonisue says. "We really pride ourselves on being the beader's bead store."

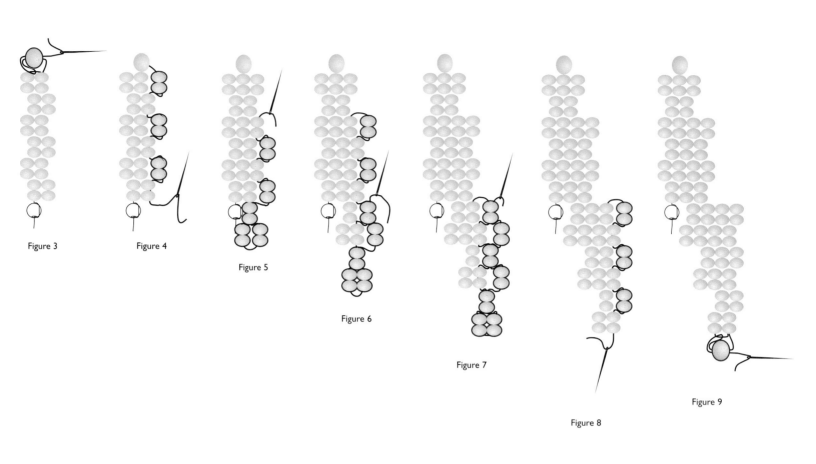

Figure 3

Figure 4

Figure 5

Figure 6

Figure 7

Figure 8

Figure 9

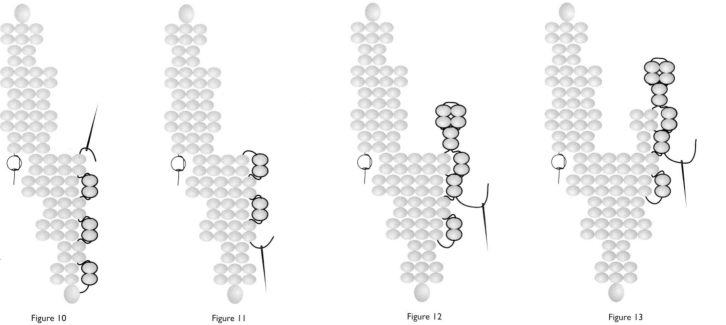

Figure 10

Figure 11

Figure 12

Figure 13

Step 4: String 1 size 8°; pass under the loop of the thread at the top and pass back through the size 8° (Figure 3).

Step 5: Repeat another row of two-drop peyote with size 11°s for a total of three stitches (Figure 4).

Step 6: Make the first increase by stringing 6 size 11°s and passing back through the second and first beads; pull taut. Make two more stitches with size 11°s (Figure 5).

Step 7: Turn and add three stitches with size 11°s. Make the increase by stringing 6 size 11°s and passing back through the second and first beads; pull taut. Make one more stitch with size 11°s (Figure 6).

Step 8: Turn and add two stitches with size 11°s. Make the third increase by stringing 6 size 11°s and passing back through the second and first beads; pull taut. Make two more stitches with size 11°s (Figure 7).

Step 9: Turn and make three stitches with size 11°s (Figure 8).

Step 10: Add 1 size 8° as in Step 4 (Figure 9).

Step 11: Make three stitches with size 11°s (Figure 10).

Step 12: Turn and make two stitches with size 11°s (Figure 11).

Step 13: Turn and make two stitches with size 11°s, make the first increase on this point by stringing 6 size 11°s and passing back through

the second and first beads; pull taut. Make one more stitch with size 11°s. (Figure 12.)

Step 14: Turn and make two stitches with size 11°s; make the second increase on this point by stringing 6 size 11°s and passing back through the second and first beads; pull taut. Make one more stitch with size 11°s. (Figure 13.)

Step 15: Repeat Steps 8–14 for a total of nine points on each side. Create the last (tenth) point like the first point in that it is only half the size of the others: repeat Steps 8–11, but only add two stitches in Step 11. (Figure 14.)

Step 16: To make the closure, remove the tension bead and string enough size 11°s on the 12" (30.5 cm) tail to form a loop that will fit over your accent bead. Attach the loop and reinforce a couple of times (Figure 15a). At the other end, string 1 size 11°, 1 accent bead, 1 size 8°, and pass back through the accent bead; pull taut. String another size 11° and attach to the bracelet. Reinforce a couple of times, knot and trim the thread close. (Figure 15b.)

Step 17: Repeat Steps 1–16 for another bracelet using the second color of size 11°s and accent beads. To join the two pieces, turn one piece over and weave the two together with the loops at one end and accent beads at the other.

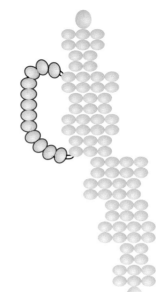

Figure 15a

Figure 15b

Figure 14

The Bead Factory

3019 Sixth Ave.
Tacoma, WA 98406
(253) 572-5529
info@thebeadfactory.com
www.thebeadfactory.com

When you walk through the doors of The Bead Factory you may feel as if you're stepping into a high-end department store—but instead of clothing you'll find a shop filled to the brim with beads. Founded by Viki and Mark Lareau in 1992 as a modest 300-square-foot shop, The Bead Factory has since expanded five times and has now settled into a 5,000-square-foot space that houses a retail store, wholesale mail-order department, three classrooms, offices, a kids' playroom, and even an area for patient spouses to relax.

The Bead Factory offers a special bead club registry, where regular customers can register to earn $10 in free merchandise for every $100 they spend, along with invitations to member-only events, including monthly group meetings and "bead and breakfast" get-togethers.

Beaders can choose from more than fifty classes each month, ranging from lampworking, Precious Metal Clay, metalsmithing, and wireworking to knotting, stringing, and beadweaving. Students with an entrepreneurial spirit have the opportunity to learn the business side of jewelry making, including all the tips bead artists need to turn their favorite hobby into profit.

"The most important element of our store is service," says Viki. "I have an exceptional staff who knows the customer comes first. I've worked hard to create a family here, and I know customers feel that when they come in. You get back what you give, it's that simple."

Classy Crystal Clusters

Carrie Hamm

Carrie chose bicone crystals for the central design element of these earrings because of the overwhelming popularity of crystals and the sparkle they add to accessories. If you find that you can't stop after making one cluster, create several for a bracelet or just add chain for a lovely three-dimensional necklace.

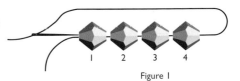

Figure 1

Materials for Ruby Clusters
  28 fuchsia 4mm Swarovski crystal bicones
  2 fuchsia 8mm Swarovski crystal bicones
  2 gold-filled eye pins
  2 gold-filled head pins
  1 pair of gold-filled French ear wires
    with balls
  Size D beading thread in color to
    complement beads

Materials for Cool Blue Clusters
  28 blue 4mm Swarovski crystal bicones
  2 Montana blue 10mm freshwater pearls
  2 sterling silver eye pins
  2 sterling silver head pins
  1 pair of sterling silver spiral ear wires
  Size D beading thread in color to
    complement beads

Tools
  Size 12 beading needle
  Round-nose pliers
  Wire cutters
  Clear nail polish

Techniques
  Wireworking, right-angle weave, gluing

Finished Size
  Ruby Clusters 1⅝" (4.1 cm);
    Blue Clusters 2" (5 cm)

Ruby Clusters

Step 1: String four 4mm bicones, leave a 10" (25.5 cm) tail, and pass through the first bead again (Figure 1).

Step 2: Pull the thread tight to form a diamond and pass through each bead again counterclockwise until you are coming out of the third bead (Figure 2).

Step 3: String 3 pink 4mm bicones and pass through the third bead again; pull tight (Figure 3).

Step 4: Pass through the beads added in Step 3 and the third bead in a clockwise direction until you come out of the sixth bead (Figure 4).

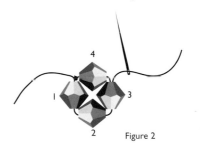

Figure 2

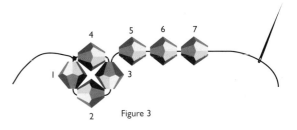

Figure 3

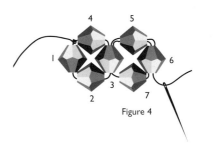

Figure 4

Step 5: String three 4mm bicones and pass through the sixth bead again; pull tight (Figure 5).

Step 6: Pass through the beads added in Step 5 and the sixth bead in a counterclockwise direction until you exit out of the ninth bead (Figure 6).

Step 7: String one 4mm bicone, pass through the top of the first bead; do not pull tight yet. String one 4mm bicone and pass through the bottom of the ninth bead. Slowly pull tight to form a cluster (Figure 7).

> ## *TIPS*
>
> ### Cleaning Swarovski Crystals and Czech Glass Beads
>
> ✔ To clean vintage or dirty Swarovski crystals and Czech glass beads, take a pair of nylon pantyhose, cut the foot off, place the beads inside the foot, close the opening by tying the end, and place in the top rack of the dishwasher. The crystals clean up beautifully and you'll save a lot of time.
>
> —Bead Works Inc.
>
> ### Threading Your Needle
>
> ✔ If you are having difficulty threading your needle, turn it 180 degrees and try again—one side of the eye's needle may be easier to thread due to the factory process of forming and punching.
>
> —Creative Castle
>
> ### Closing Head Pin Loops
>
> ✔ Use the top slot of a crimping tool to tightly close head pin loops.
>
> —Bead Angels Bead Shop

Step 8: Continue passing the needle and thread through the beads to reinforce the cluster until it feels firm. Tie a knot between two beads and secure with clear nail polish. Pass through an adjacent bead and trim the thread close; repeat with the tail.

Step 9: Slide an 8mm bicone on a gold-filled eye pin. Bend the wire at a 90-degree angle directly above the bead, trim the wire to about ¼" (6 mm), and using the round-nose pliers, make a simple loop and set aside.

Step 10: Slide one 4mm bicone, the center of the cluster, and another pink 4mm bicone on a gold-filled head pin. Trim and loop the wire as in Step 9.

Step 11: Open both the simple loop created in Step 9 and the loop of the eye pin, connect one loop to a gold-filled ear wire, and connect the other to the loop of the cluster; close the loops (Figure 8).

Step 12: Repeat Steps 1–11 for a second earring.

Cool Blue Clusters

Step 1: Repeat Steps 1–12 above using the blue 4mm bicones in place of the fuchsia 4mm bicones, the 10mm pearls in place of the 8mm bicones, and the sterling silver ear wires, eye pins, and head pins for a second pair of earrings.

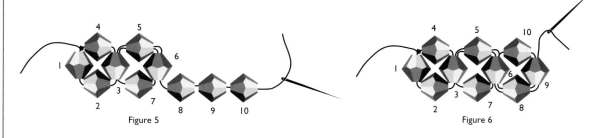

Figure 5

Figure 6

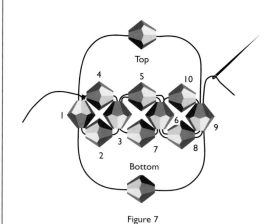

Figure 7

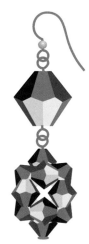

Figure 8

Stretchy Button Vines

● ● ● ● ● ● ● ● ● ● ● ● ● ●

Melissa Cable

Before pursuing her dream to open a bead store, Melissa worked for the state's oldest winery, Chateau Ste. Michelle. The vineyards that were once part of her daily routine inspired the "vines" that float from one button to the next in this bracelet. Her sister-in-law Tiffany, who made the pictured bracelet, took advantage of bold purple buttons and seed beads to produce a fun-to-wear, playful accessory. Shake your wrist and listen to the buttons click.

Materials
7 g amethyst luster size 11° Japanese seed beads
7 g maroon striped size 6° seed beads
2 g purple size 8° Japanese seed beads
20 amethyst 4–6mm Swarovski crystal bicones
40 light, medium, and dark purple 10–15mm buttons
9" (23 cm) of 1mm stretch cord
Size D beading thread in color to complement beads

Tools
Size 12 beading needle

Technique
Stringing

Finished Size
8" (20.5 cm) in diameter

Note: The assorted button mix is available from Junkitz; (732) 792-1108; www.junkitz.com.

Step 1: *Base.* Stretch the cord by giving it a few good strong pulls. String enough size 6°s (these are known as "base" beads) to make a bracelet that is comfortable to you. Tie a knot tightly three times (the knot will be hidden inside one of the base beads). Tie the thread around the cord between two base beads, leaving a 6" (15 cm) tail, being sure not to tie the thread so tightly that it cuts through the cord. Feed the end of the tail through a few of the base beads on the left side; pull the needle and thread through the first base bead to the right of the thread knot. The rest of the bracelet is made up of sections that include two button vines and one crystal connector vine; the vines are different heights for variety. *Note:* The key to this bracelet is that no two base beads are ever sewn together; instead, the crystal connector vines float above the base beads, allowing the bracelet to stretch.

this project is from

Beadclub

17616 140th Ave. NE
Woodinville, WA 98072
(425) 949-1080
info@beadclub.com
www.beadclub.com

Looking to join the ultimate club? Then don't miss Beadclub in Woodinville, Washington. Founded in July of 2003 by mother-daughter team Melissa Cable and Bonnie Robinius, Beadclub is geared to beaders who want to learn. Students will find an array of classes at this clutter-free shop, ranging from basic knotting, stringing, wirewrapping, and Precious Metal Clay, to two-hour "instant gratification" classes where students leave with a finished project. Even kids get special treatment: children ages five and up are encouraged to sign up for classes and private parties.

There's never a dull moment at this shop. Beadclub's creative "bead and feed" special events feature dinner and beverages while students work on projects. Kitclub, where customers receive quarterly bracelet kits in the mail, keeps beaders up-to-date with the newest seasonal colors and trends. And every Monday night is "drop-in" night, a time for students to get a quick lesson or help with a technique or project.

Since 2004, Beadclub customers volunteer their time to make special bracelets to raise money for the Melanoma International Foundation (MIF). As of 2006, over 1,000 bracelets have been strung and $5,000 has been raised. Many of Beadclub's customers walk for "Team Beadclub" in Seattle's Annual Safe in the Shade walk-a-thon benefiting MIF.

Customers also stay connected with the shop's friendly atmosphere through the Internet—Beadclub allows beaders to create personal gallery pages linked to the store's main webpage. Emerging artists use this as a way to archive their work, share their designs with friends, and sell original creations.

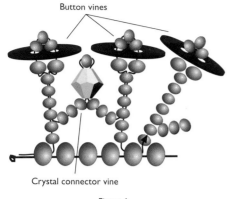

Button vines

Crystal connector vine

Figure 1

Step 2: *First button vine.* String 5–8 size 11°s, 1 size 8°, and through one hole of one button. String 3–4 size 11°s (string enough to cover the space between the holes in the button; you may need more if your beads slip through the holes). Pass the needle through the second hole in the button and string 1 size 8°. Pass back through all of the size 11°s except the last two before the base bead. (Figure 1.)

Step 3: *Crystal connector vines.* String 3 size 11°s, 1 crystal, and 1 size 11°. Pass back through the crystal and string 3 size 11°s. (Figure 1.)

Step 4: *Second button vine.* String 3–6 (depending on how far you wish the button to hang away from the base beads) size 11°s, 1 size 8°, and through one hole of one button. String 4 size 11°s (or enough to cover the space between the holes in the button). Pass through the second hole in the button and string 1 size 8°. Pass back through all the size 11°s except the last 3 before the crystal. String 2 size 11°s and pass through the fifth base bead, skipping over

VARIATION The green bracelet, made by Melissa Cable, is a simple variation on the purple bracelet. String the base with dark green matte size 6° seed beads and substitute the purple seed beads with dark and light olive green buttons and shades of olive green size 11° and 8° seed beads. String the crystal connector vines with dark amethyst matte AB size 11° seed beads. *Top the first connector vine with a 6mm olivine Swarovski bicone crystal and a button vine. String the second connector vine with a 6mm amethyst Swarovski bicone and a button vine. To string each third connector vine, string 3 amethyst size 11°s, one 4mm olivine Swarovski bicone, and 1 amethyst size 11°; pass back through the olivine bicone and string a 4mm amethyst Swarovski bicone and an amethyst size 11°; pass back through the amethyst bicone and string 3 more amethyst size 11°s. Repeat from * around.

The shell bracelet, made by Pam Brown, is an elegant, dressed up version of the purple bracelet. String the base with crystal beige-lined size 6° seed beads. Top the crystal vine connectors with an assortment of 6mm topaz and peridot 6mm Swarovski crystals, 6mm beige pearls, and pink 10mm bell flower shaped beads. Instead of stringing all the button vines as directed in Step 2, make some by stringing 5 size 11° beige seed beads, 1 vermeil 4mm spacer, 2 beige size 11°s, 1 topaz AB size 8° seed bead, 1 hole of a large button, 1 beige size 11°, 1 hole of a smaller button, a vermeil bead cap, and 1 beige size 11°; pass back through the bead cap and into the other hole of the small button, 1 beige size 11°, and the other hole of the larger button; string 1 topaz size 8°; pass back through the two beige size 11°s, the spacer and two beige size 11°s, and prepare to make the next crystal vine connector. Vary the topping on each button, making some with two size 11°s, a vermeil spacer, and two more size 11°s.

Consider making a fuller bracelet by skipping only two beads between the button vines (instead of three as directed for the purple bracelet) or by working another round into the base beads. If you wish for the bracelet to be less full, skip more than three beads between the button vines and lengthen the crystal connector vines by adding 4–5 size 11°s on each side of the crystal (instead of just three).

Green bracelet variation

Shell bracelet variation

the second, third, and fourth base beads.
(Figure 1.)

Step 5: *Finishing.* Repeat Steps 1–4 until you
reach the first base bead; if you do not end
exactly where you started and have less
than five base beads remaining, skip the second button vine in the last section and
attach the crystal connector vine to the first
button vine by passing the needle back
through the two size 11°s closest to the
base beads of the first button vine. If you
just have two or three base beads left, simply make a crystal connector between your
last button vine and the first button vine.
To end the thread, pass the needle and
thread through the first few connectors and
button vines, make 2–3 half hitch knots, and
trim the thread close; repeat with the tail,
working in the opposite direction.

The Bead Cache

3307 S. College Ave., Ste. 105
Fort Collins, CO 80525
(970) 224-4322

When Heidi Gore first began beading fifteen years ago, she didn't think there was much to the bead universe beyond structured loomwork in size 11° and 15° seed beads. Since then, her outlook on the craft has completely changed. "I'm struck by the diversity of beadwork now, the free-form beadwork, and all the new trends and ideas," she says.

Heidi began her beading career by creating loomworked hat bands for a custom hat shop in Durango, Colorado. From there she went on to manage a small bead shop, where she gained the experience and expertise she needed to open her very own bead shop years later.

Heidi opened The Bead Cache in cozy Old Town Fort Collins, Colorado, in 1997. Six years later, when the shop outgrew its original setting, it moved just three miles away to a new location near a yarn shop and a popular natural foods market. The class roster now includes forty different classes on an array of techniques including Precious Metal Clay, seed bead stitches, and jewelry incorporating textiles. Bead parties and a jewelry repair business also keep the store and its staff busy and thriving. Designer Keriann Gore, Heidi's daughter, is the backbone of the shop: she teaches classes, manages inventory, travels to bead shows, repairs jewelry, and—most important—dreams up plenty of original beaded creations.

The Bead Cache stocks seed beads, semiprecious stones, vintage beads, Czech glass beads, tools, findings, sterling silver and gold-filled beads, designer beads, African trade beads, and more. Special events include workshops taught by nationally known teachers like lampworker Alethia Donathan from Honolulu, Hawaii.

Collage Carryall
● ● ● ● ● ● ● ● ● ●

Keriann Gore

This cigar box purse is a quick and easy project that functions as a trendy accessory and a hip way to tote materials to your next beading class. Keriann's dogs, who frequent the shop, inspired this project. Personalize your own tote with favorite photographs and postcards.

Materials
16 cream gilt-lined size 11° Japanese seed beads
25 green transparent size 11° Japanese seed beads
60 teal matte size 11° Japanese seed beads
4 turquoise 15mm porcelain disks
4 turquoise 12×37mm porcelain rectangles
6 red 12mm skunk beads
12 white 7–10mm ostrich shell rondelles
15 red 5mm vintage clover sequins
16 brass 5mm spacers
4 sterling silver 2×2mm crimp tubes
Size D beading thread in color to complement beads
18" (45.5 cm) of .024 beading wire
3 postcards, pictures, and/or printed papers
1 cigar box
Outdoor Mod Podge
2 pieces black 1½×⅜" (3.8×1 cm) suede leather
4 steel ⅜" (1 cm) wood screws

Tools
Size 12 beading needle
Crimping pliers
Wire cutter
1" (2.5 cm) wide sponge brush
Screwdriver

Technique
Stringing

Finished Size
6¾×7¼×3¾" (17×18.5×9.5 cm) box;
13½" (34.5 cm) handle

Note: Cigar boxes and Outdoor Mod Podge are available at craft stores or online resources; visit your local cigar store for a genuine cigar box.

Cigar Box

Step 1: Using the clovers, seed beads, and four brass spacers, embellish two of your images. To create the flowers: bring the needle up through the ground material (one of the photographs, postcards, or pieces of paper), string 4 green size 11°s, 1 clover, 1 cream size 11°, pass back through the clover and 2 green size 11°s, string 1 green size 11°, 1 clover, 1 cream size 11°s, and pass back through the clover and 3 green size 11°s before taking the needle to the back of the ground material; flowers can also be made by omitting some or all of the green size 11°s or clovers. Using the assorted beads, embellish elements of the ground material as desired: the dog's collar was made by stringing 14 brown size 15° Japanese seed beads and 1 blue size 15° Japanese seed bead for the tag. The photograph of the sign was embellished in each corner by bringing the needle up, stringing 1 brass spacer, 1 teal size 11°, and passing back through the brass spacer before taking the needle to the back.

Step 2: Trim the images to the size and shape desired, ensuring they are smaller than the front of the box.

Step 3: Using the sponge brush and the side of the cigar box with the closure facing up, paint Outdoor Mod Podge on the back of all the pieces and place them on the cigar box as desired. Allow to completely dry.

Step 4: Once dry, paint the Outdoor Mod Podge on the cigar box, covering the entire box and images and trying not to heavily coat the beads. Allow to dry completely.

> ### TIPS
> **Prevent Spilled Beads**
> ✔ If you don't have a bead stopper or alligator clip to hold beads in place while stringing, use a hemostat clamp on each end of the beading wire.
>
> **Organizing Your Stash**
> ✔ Sort beads in your bead boxes by color, not by size or type—it will be easier to choose a palette for your project when your colors are together and encourage you to experiment with combining beads of different sizes, textures, and materials.
> —*Beadissimo*

Handle

Step 5: Using two wood screws, the screwdriver, and working on the side of the cigar box with the closure, attach one piece of leather: center the piece front to back and 1¼" (3.2 cm) from one side and pinch the center of the leather to create a loop; screw in place (the screws will be about ⅛" [3 mm] from the ends of the leather and 12 mm from each other). Repeat with the remaining piece of leather of the other side of the box.

Step 6: Using the beading wire, string 28 teal size 11°s, 2 crimp tubes, and pass through one leather loop. Pass back through the two crimp tubes, crimp both crimp tubes, and trim the tail of the wire close.

Step 7: *String 1 disk, 1 spacer, 1 ostrich shell, 1 skunk bead, 1 ostrich shell, 1 spacer, 1 rectangular bead, 1 spacer, 1 ostrich shell, 1 skunk bead, 1 ostrich shell, and 1 spacer. Repeat from * and string 1 disk.

Step 8: String 2 crimp tubes, 28 teal size 11°s, pass through the second leather loop, pass back through the two crimp tubes, and pull tight. Crimp both crimp tubes and trim the

Teardrops and Ruffles Beaded Beads Bracelets

Grazyna Rurka and Suzin Skyler Hein

Designed and created by Grazyna, a Calgary artist who regularly teaches her original designs at Suzie Q Beads, both the Teardrops and Ruffles beaded beads begin with a base worked on a dowel in tubular right-angle weave. Once the base is formed, the beads are embellished. Shop owner Suzin strung these fun bracelets incorporating Grazyna's dynamic hand-made beads.

Materials for Triangle Teardrops
Beaded Beads and Bracelet
  3 g each of light, medium, and dark brown
    size 11° Japanese seed beads
  5 g dark brown metallic 3mm
    Japanese teardrops
  22 Bali silver 6mm round beads
  11 Bali silver 8×1mm spacers
  1 sterling silver box clasp
  2 sterling silver 2×2mm crimp tubes
  Size D beading thread in color to
    complement beads
  11" (28 cm) of .019 beading wire

Materials for Ruffles
Beaded Beads and Bracelet
  6 g lime green size 11° Japanese seed beads
  1 g orange size 11° Japanese seed beads
  7 g lime green size 10° Miyuki triangle beads
  2 lime green 4mm faceted rondelles
  4 orange 15×18mm oval acrylic beads
  8 silver 6mm bead caps
  2 filigree 10mm silver round beads
  1 sterling silver box clasp
  2 sterling silver 2×2mm crimp tubes
  Size D beading thread in color to
    complement beads
  11" (28 cm) of .019 beading wire

Tools
  Size 12 beading needle
  1 dowel about 4mm in diameter and 1 about
    6mm in diameter

Techniques
  Tubular right-angle weave, stringing, crimping
Finished Size
  Triangle Teardrop Beaded Beads, 17×10mm (one
    side) and Bracelet, 8¾" (22 cm); Ruffle Beaded
    Beads, 17×17mm and Bracelet, 9" (23 cm)

Tubular Right-Angle Weave Base

Step 1: *Notes:* Both beaded beads begin with the Tubular Right-Angle Weave Base. Follow the general instructions here when forming the base as indicated in Step 1 below for the Triangle Teardrop and Step 1 below for the Ruffle. String 4 size 11°s and tie the threads together in a knot, making a circle; bring the needle up through next bead (Figure 1).

Figure 1

this project is from
Suzie Q Beads

1207 Tenth Ave. SE
Calgary, AB, Canada T2G 0W6
(403) 266-1202
suzieqbeads@shaw.ca
www.suzieqbeads.com

Even before you step through the doors of the orange and chartreuse house that is home to Suzie Q Beads, and you see it is a truly unique bead boutique—the chartreuse beaded Volvo parked out front indicates that this isn't a run-of-the-mill business!

Owner Suzin Skyler Hein credits her "craft girl" beginnings with the creation of Suzie Q Beads, which opened in 2002. The shop, she says, is for both beginners and the already bead-obsessed. "I absolutely love what I'm doing with my bead store," she says. "Seeking out fabulous beads for my wonderful customers, inspiring and educating them . . . it's so much fun. I'm passionately dedicated to fostering the art of beading."

The shop, which doubles as a workshop and gallery, carries a large selection of beading books, tools, findings, wire, and sterling silver, Czech pressed glass, vintage, semiprecious, and Japanese seed beads. Classes are offered in introductory jewelry making, wireworking, beadweaving, bead crochet, bead knitting, beaded beads, and bead embroidery.

Suzin's bead obsession isn't limited to the beads in her shop: by the time the engine gave out, about one third of her first car, a 1984 Saab (also known as Mr. SLABB), was covered in beads, including a jewel-encrusted crown on the top. Although the Saab was retired, it is still parked behind the shop, and Suzin has a new shop mascot—the beaded Volvo, which she has named Mr. Bead. "Mr. Bead has fewer beads than his predecessor but looks way better design-wise in the way the beads are being attached, so I think of Mr. SLABB as my practice car," she says. "Everywhere we go, we always get a lot of attention!"

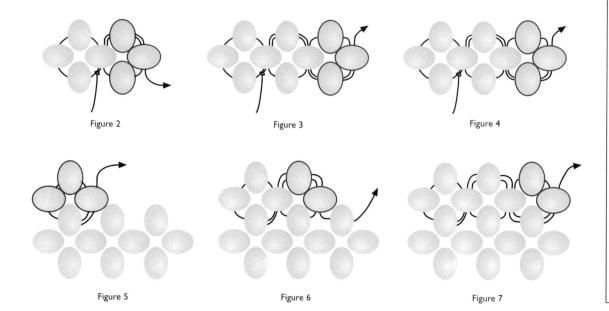

Figure 2   Figure 3   Figure 4

Figure 5   Figure 6   Figure 7

Step 2: String 3 size 11°s and working clockwise, bring the needle up through the same bead it is exiting, forming a circle. Continue around through the top bead and down through the side bead. (Figure 2.)

Step 3: String 3 size 11°s and work as in Step 2 but working counterclockwise; you now have three units (Figure 3).

Step 4: Repeat Steps 2–3 for a total of five units if making the Triangle Teardrop. Repeat Steps 2–3 for a total of seven units if making the Ruffle.

Step 5: Wrap the units around the 4mm dowel if making the Triangle Teardrop or around the 6mm dowel if making the Ruffle, with the tail of the thread hanging down and the working thread coming up out of the side bead in the last unit. To join the sixth unit for the Triangle Teardrop (or eighth unit for the Ruffle) to the first unit, string 1 bead, bring the needle down

through first side bead of the first unit, string another bead, bring the needle up through the side bead of the fifth unit for the Triangle Teardrop (or the seventh for the Ruffle), and continue through the top bead. Pass through these four beads again to ensure the row is secure. (Figure 4.)

Step 6: Work in tubular right-angle weave for one more row for the Triangle Teardrop (or three more rows for the Ruffle). The subsequent row(s) consists of 3 size 11°s to form the first unit (Figure 5), 2 size 11°s to form the second through fifth units if making the Triangle Teardrop (or the second through seventh units if working the Ruffle) alternating between working clockwise and counterclockwise as required (Figure 6), and 1 size 11° to form the sixth and final unit of each row if making the Triangle Teardrop (or the eighth and final unit if making the Ruffle) (Figure 7).

Triangle Teardrop Beaded Bead

Step 1: Following Steps 1–6 above for the Tubular Right-Angle Weave Base, using 36" (91.5 cm) of beading thread, and leaving a tail about 6" (15 cm) long, make the Tubular Right-Angle Weave Base consisting of six units and two rows with the light brown size 11°s on the 4mm dowel.

Step 2: With the thread coming out of a top bead, string 3 size 11°s and pass through the next top bead in the row, forming a picot. Keep tension tight and make sure the beads fit snugly between each size 11°. (Figure 8.)

Step 3: Repeat Step 2 five more times for a total of six picots. When completing the last picot, bring the thread up through the first two beads of the first picot.

Step 4: String 1 size 11°, 1 teardrop bead, 1 size 11°, and pass through the middle bead of the next picot. Continue through the

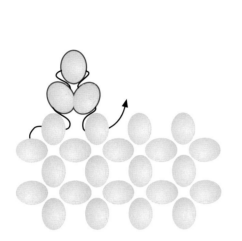

Figure 8

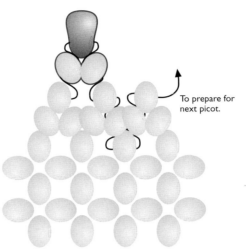

To prepare for next picot.

Figure 9

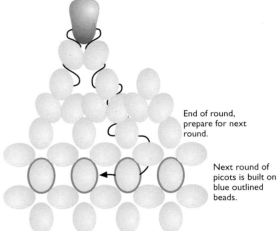

End of round, prepare for next round.

Next round of picots is built on blue outlined beads.

Figure 10

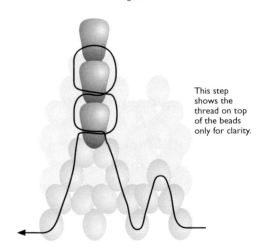

This step shows the thread on top of the beads only for clarity.

Figure 11

third bead of the second picot, the top bead of the base row, and the first two beads of the third picot. (Figure 9.)

Step 5: Repeat Step 4 two more times. The picots begin to form a triangle shape. (You should have a second set of picots between the first and second, third and fourth, and fifth and sixth picots of the first set of picots formed in Steps 1–2.)

Step 6: Weave the needle down through the middle row and come out one of the size 11°s with a hole facing horizontally (Figure 10).

Step 7: String 3 size 11°s and pass through the next size 11° in the row, forming a picot. Keep tension tight and make sure the beads fit snugly between each size 11°. Repeat to the end of the row for a total of six picots. When completing the last picot, bring the thread up through the first two beads of the first picot.

Step 8: Repeat Steps 4–5, matching placement of the second set of picots in this row to those formed in the previous row.

Step 9: Weave the needle down through to bottom row and come out of one of the size 11°s with a hole facing horizontally in the same manner as Step 6.

Step 10: Repeat Steps 7–8.

Step 11: Continue through to the next teardrop bead in the row and pass through the teardrop bead. Weave through the three teardrops in a figure-eight pattern to anchor them together; continue to the next two teardrop bead formations and repeat (Figure 11).

Step 12: Repeat Step 11 through the middle and top row for strength. Remove the dowel.

Step 13: Weave the tails through several of the size 11°s in the base and trim the threads close.

TIP Opposites Attract

✔ Use a contrast of dark and light, matte and shiny, and round and square beads to enhance your design. Mixing and matching shapes, sizes, textures, and colors will make your jewelry all the more interesting.

—The Bead Shop

Step 14: Repeat Steps 1–13 nine times, using the light brown size 11's for 2 more beaded beads, medium brown size 11's for 4 beaded beads, and dark brown size 11's for 3 beaded beads.

Step 15: To string the bracelet, string the beading wire through a crimp tube, a round silver bead, one end of the clasp, and back through the round silver bead and the crimp tube. Crimp the tube and trim the end of the wire close. *String 1 spacer, 1 round bead, 1 dark brown beaded bead, and 1 round bead. Repeat from * nine times alternating the shades of brown beaded beads. String 1 spacer, 1 crimp tube, 1 round bead, and the other side of the clasp. Pass back through the round bead and the crimp tube. Crimp the tube and trim the end of the wire close.

Ruffle Beaded Bead

Step 1: Following Steps 1–6 above for the Tubular Right-Angle Weave Base, using 48" (122 cm) of beading thread, and leaving a tail about 6" (15 cm) long, make the Tubular Right-Angle Weave Base consisting of eight units and four rows with lime green size 11° round beads. *Note:* To form the Ruffle bead, you will be making a picot between the five rows of beads in the base with the hole sitting horizontally (as indicated by the blue outlined beads in Figure 12) when you hold the needle or dowel vertically. (Figure 12.)

Step 2: Place the tube on the 4mm dowel.

Step 3: With the thread coming out of a top (or "up") bead in the last row, string 3 triangle beads and pass through the next top bead in the row, forming a picot. Keep tension tight and make sure the beads form a picot between each size 11° (Figure 13).

Step 4: Repeat Step 3 seven more times around the row for a total of eight picots. Weave the thread down through the vertical bead hole directly under the last picot and pass thread through a horizontal bead hole.

Step 5: *String 3 lime green size 11's between each size 11° horizontal bead (eight picots) in the second "horizontal" row of beads (see note in Step 1 above). Pull snugly and weave the thread down to the next horizontal row of beads. String 1 lime green, 1 orange, and 1 lime green size 11° when filling the space between the next horizontal beads of the band. Repeat from * while working across the row. (Figure 14.)

Step 6: Repeat Step 3–4 in the third horizontal row.

Step 7: Repeat Step 5 in the fourth horizontal row.

Step 8: Repeat Step 6 in the fifth horizontal row. Remove the dowel.

Step 9: Weave the tail and working thread through several of the size 11's in the base and trim the threads close.

Step 10: Repeat Steps 1–9 four more times.

Step 11: To string the bracelet, string the beading wire through a crimp tube, a green rondelle, one end of the clasp, and back through the green rondelle and the crimp tube. Crimp the tube and trim the end of the wire close. String 1 silver filigree round bead, *1 beaded bead, 1 bead cap, 1 orange oval, and 1 bead cap. Repeat from * three times. String 1 beaded bead, 1 silver filigree round bead, 1 crimp tube, 1 green rondelle, and the other side of the clasp. Pass back through the green rondelle and the crimp tube. Crimp the tube and trim the end of the wire close.

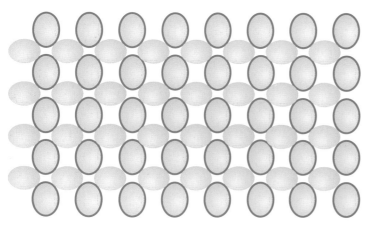

Figure 12
The rounds of picots are built on the blue outlined beads.

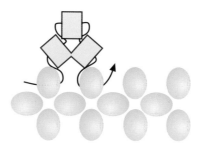

Figure 13

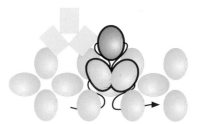

Figure 14

Frida
● ● ● ●

Beth Kraft

Beth was inspired by Mexican artist Frida Kahlo's sense of bold color when creating this bracelet. The bracelet features small elements made with a variety of bead techniques, including rings made with tubular herringbone stitch and fringe, that are strung together with unique beads for a bright juxtaposition of color. Create your own original bracelet based on your favorite artist's color palette or artwork.

Materials
- 12 yellow size 11° Delicas
- 5 g clear aqua-lined size 11° Japanese seed beads
- 5 g red silver-lined size 11° Japanese seed beads
- 5 g orange opaque size 11° Japanese seed beads
- 28 yellow size 8° Japanese seed beads
- 18 magenta AB 3×4mm teardrops
- 46 light blue clear 3×4mm teardrops
- 2 light orange 8×15mm glass teardrops
- 1 light orange 13×15mm vintage glass heart bead
- 1 red 7×16mm glass vintage crescent bead
- 1 red 10×18mm glass vintage tapered barrel bead
- 4 teal and gold 15×3mm glass rondelles
- 1 gold matte 6×2mm ceramic ring
- 1 light teal 6×2mm rondelle
- 1 red AB 20×3mm lampworked button with 1 hole
- 1 clear teal-lined 10×10mm furnace glass bead
- 1 red oval 9×4mm glass horizontally drilled oval
- 1 red 6×9mm pressed-glass spiral bead
- 1 frosted clear with orange tips 13×17mm vintage twisted bead
- 1 orange 7×6mm triangle lampworked bead
- 3 teal 10×4mm teardrop beads
- 1 red, orange, purple, and black 9×13mm lampworked barrel bead
- 1 clear and teal 21×3mm large-holed furnace glass disk
- 1 light orange 9×7mm bow-shaped bead
- 1 orange, blue, and red 18mm lampworked round bead
- 1 blue, orange, red, lime green, and peach clear 8×18mm vertically drilled lampworked disk
- 1 teal matte 4×8mm pressed-glass barrel
- 2 sterling silver 2×2mm crimp tube
- Fireline 6 lb test thread
- 22" (56 cm) of .014 beading wire
- Clear nail polish

Tools
- Size 12 beading needle
- Wire cutters
- Crimping pliers

Techniques
- Fringe, stringing, tubular herringbone

Finished Size
8¾" (22 cm)

Note: The red lampworked button is available from Bronwen Heilman, Ghost Cow Glassworks; (520) 622-7199; www.ghostcow.com. The 18mm lampworked round bead is available from Cathy Collison, Glass Garden Beads; (507) 645-0301; www.glassgardenbeads.com. The 8×18mm lampworked disk is available from Sue Peoples; www.peoplesbeaddreams.com. If you are unable to find the beads used in this project, choose favorite beads from your stash, including antique and lampworked beads.

TIP Before Crimping
✔ Remember to always remove the slack in the wire before crimping.
—International Glass & Bead Company

---

this project is from

Nordic Gypsy Beads and Jewelry

20 Third St. SW
Rochester, MN 55902
(507) 288-2258
web@nordicgypsy.com
www.nordicgypsy.com

Nordic Gypsy Beads and Jewelry is just the place to visit for inspiration served up with a bit of energy, attitude, and humor. Located in downtown Rochester, Minnesota, within walking distance of the Mayo Clinic and nestled in between a few antique stores on historic Third Street, this truly special shop provides a comforting space to bead. "We find a way to make everyone have fun," says owner Beth Kraft. Beth was a customer herself, taking classes and shopping at the store frequently, until she and her husband Curt decided to buy it. "People want classes that make them feel successful and happy. We offer a welcoming, comforting space to relax and unwind."

The shop's upbeat attitude has a bit to do with the neighborhood—visitors of the Mayo Clinic from around the world may stop in looking for a place to loosen up after a tough day. Nordic Gypsy's staff is always willing to help new beaders, who may feel overwhelmed at the prospect of selecting a few beads, or advanced beaders looking for a little insight.

The extensive bead selection includes vintage, stone, Swarovski, Bali, Thai, and African beads, Czech and Japanese seed beads, and Delicas, as well as findings, pearls, tools, and books. The shop offers unusual classes, and the staff relishes participating in extraordinary beading instruction, like when staff members taught beading to 200 wild Girl Scouts at a "lock-in."

"We love to play at work," Beth says. Her advice? "Don't be afraid to make mistakes, just make sure you're having a good time."

Drop Rings

Step 1: Working with the needle and Fireline, string 1 yellow Delica and 1 light blue teardrop six times. Pass through all of the beads at least three times to reinforce. Tie a square knot and seal by touching the knot with a needle tip dipped in nail polish. Trim the threads close. (Figure 1.) Set aside.

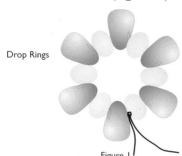

Drop Rings

Figure 1

Step 2: Repeat Step 1 for one more ring.

Step 3: Repeat Step 1 with assorted-colored size 11°s and teardrops.

Tubular Herringbone Bead Ring

Step 1: Count out 36 red silver-lined size 11°s (this will keep you from having to count each row). *Note:* The ring is worked in "speedy" tubular herringbone stitch, called "speedy" because two rows are worked at the same time. Working with the needle and Fireline, begin the ladder-stitch base by stringing 2 of the red silver-lined size 11°s and 2 orange opaque size 11°s. Lay the beads out with a 6" (15 cm) tail exiting on the left. Pass through the red silver-lined size 11°s again from the left to the right.

Pass back through the orange size 11°s from the right to the left. String 2 clear aqua-lined size 11°s and pass through the orange size 11°s from the left to the right. Pass back through the clear aqua-lined size 11°s from the right to the left. String 2 clear aqua-lined size 11°s and pass through the previous clear aqua-lined size 11°s from the left to the right. Pass back through the new clear aqua-lined size 11°s from the right to the left. Join the ladder into a square by passing through the red silver-lined size 11°s from the left to the right and pass back through the clear aqua-lined size 11°s from the right to the left. Pass through the red silver-lined size 11°s one more time to correctly position the needle.

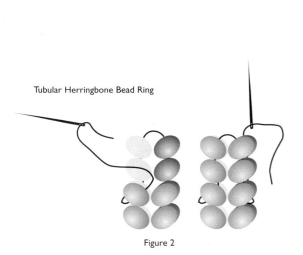

Tubular Herringbone Bead Ring

Figure 2

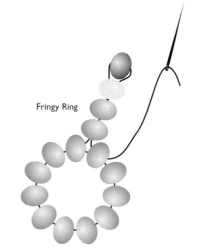

Fringy Ring

Figure 3

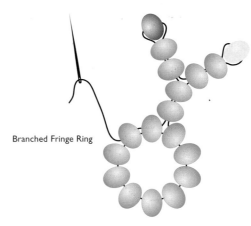

Branched Fringe Ring

Figure 4a

Step 2: Hold the square with the thread tail at the bottom and the working thread at the top. With the thread exiting the red silver-lined size 11°, *string 2 red silver-lined size 11°s and 2 orange opaque size 11°s. Pass through the top orange opaque size 11° in the square from the top. Pass through the clear aqua-lined size 11° from the bottom of the bead so the needle exits at the top of the square. String 4 clear aqua-lined size 11°s, and pass through the bottom of the next clear aqua-lined size 11°. (Figure 2.) Pass through the bottom of the three red silver-lined size 11°s so the thread is exiting the top red silver-lined size 11°. Repeat from * until all 36 red silver-lined size 11°s have been used.

Step 3: Twist one end of the tube one full rotation and then join the tube into a ring by passing through each corresponding color at the other end.

Step 4: Repeat from * around. Tie off, seal with a drop of nail polish and trim the threads close. Set aside.

Simple Seed Bead Rings

Step 1: Working with the needle and Fireline, string 7 yellow size 8°s and pass through all beads twice to make a ring. Tie

a square knot, seal with a drop of nail polish and trim the threads close. Set aside.

Step 2: Repeat Step 1 with 8 assorted-colored size 11°s.

Fringy Ring

Step 1: Working with the needle and Fireline, string 11 clear aqua-lined size 11°s and pass through all beads again to make a ring. Tie a square knot.

Step 2: Add fringe between each clear aqua-lined size 11° by stringing 2 clear aqua-lined size 11°s, 1 orange opaque size 11°, and 1 red silver-lined size 11°, skip the last bead strung, and pass back through the first three beads. Pass through the next bead in the ring. Continue making fringe around the ring until back to the beginning. (Figure 3.) Tie a square knot, seal with a drop of nail polish and trim the threads close. Set aside.

Branched Fringe Ring

Step 1: Working with the needle and Fireline, string 10 clear aqua-lined size 11°s and pass through all again to make a ring. Tie a square knot.

Step 2: *Add branch fringe by stringing 4 clear aqua-lined size 11°s and 1 orange opaque size 11°. Skip the orange opaque size 11°

and pass back through the next two clear aqua-lined size 11°s. String 2 clear aqua-lined size 11°s and 1 red silver-lined size 11°. Skip the red silver-lined size 11° and pass back through the two clear aqua-lined size 11°s just added, and continue through the first two clear aqua-lined size 11°s added in this step. Pass through two beads in the ring. (Figure 4a.) Repeat from * four times.

Step 3: Pass through one bead on the ring and string 10 clear aqua-lined size 11°s and 1 red silver-lined size 11°. Skip the red silver-lined size 11° and pass back through three clear aqua-lined size 11°s. String 2 clear aqua-lined size 11°s and 1 red silver-lined size 11°. Skip the red silver-lined size 11° and pass back through the two clear aqua-lined size 11°s and the next two clear aqua-lined size 11°s on the string of ten. String 4 clear aqua-lined size 11°s and 1 orange opaque size 11°. Skip the orange opaque size 11° and pass back through the next two clear aqua-lined size 11°s. String 2 clear aqua-lined size 11°s and 1 red silver-lined size 11°. Skip the red silver-lined size 11° and pass back through the two clear aqua-lined size 11°s just added, and continue through the first two clear aqua-lined size 11°s added in this step. Pass through the next two beads on the string of ten. Repeat from * two more times. (Figure 4b.) Pass through several beads of the base ring. Tie off, seal with a drop of nail polish and trim the threads close. Set aside.

Simplified Porcupine

Step 1: Working with the needle and Fireline, make a ring with 8 yellow size 8° seed beads.

Step 2: *String 4 assorted-colored size 11°s and a 3×4mm teardrop fringe bead. Pass back through the 4 size 11°s. Pass through the next size 8° in the circle. Repeat from * until around the circle.

Step 3: Repeat Step 2 three times (Figure 5). Tie a square knot, seal with a drop of nail polish and trim the threads close. Set aside.

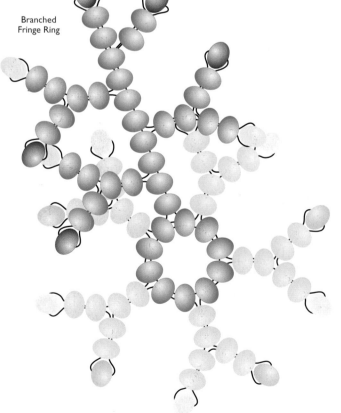

Branched Fringe Ring

Figure 4b

Stringing

Step 1: At this point, mix the remaining size 11°s together and string the colors at random. String 32 size 11°s on the beading wire and slide them to the center of the wire. String both ends of the beading wire through a crimp tube and crimp. String both ends of the wire through the Branched Fringed Ring to hide the crimp. String 1 yellow size 8°. On one end of the beading wire string 2 size 11°s, one end of the red crescent bead, 3 size 11°s, 1 yellow size 8°, 1 size 11°, the other end of the red crescent, and 2 size 11°s. On the other end of the beading wire, string 3 size 11°s, 1 light orange 8×15mm glass teardrop, 2 size 11°s, 1 teal matte 4×8mm pressed-glass barrel, and 1 size 11°.

Step 2: String both ends of the beading wire through 1 yellow size 8°, 3 teal and gold 15×3mm glass rondelles, and the Simple Seed Bead Ring made from yellow 8°s. On one end of the beading wire, string 7 size 11°s, the light orange 13×15mm glass heart bead, and 3 size 11°s. On the other end of the beading wire, string one 8×18mm vertically drilled lampworked disk and 2 size 11°s.

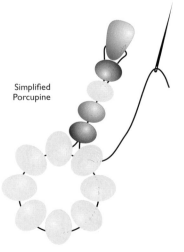

Simplified Porcupine

Figure 5

Step 3: String both ends of the beading wire through the Tubular Herringbone Bead Ring, 1 red 10×18mm glass tapered barrel bead, 2 yellow and blue Drop Rings, and one 18mm lampworked round bead. On one end of the beading wire string 1 yellow size 8°, 2 size 11°s, 2 teal 10×4mm teardrop beads, and 4 size 11°s. On the other end of the beading wire string 1 yellow size 8°, 3 size 11°s, 1 teal 10×4mm teardrop bead, 1 light orange 9×7mm bow-shaped bead, and 1 size 11°.

Step 4: String both ends of the beading wire through one 9×13mm lampworked barrel bead, 1 clear and teal 21×3mm large-holed furnace glass disk, and the Simplified Porcupine. Thread one end of the beading wire through 8 size 11°s, 1 clear teal-lined 10×10mm furnace glass bead, and 3 size 11°s. On the other end of the beading wire, string 2 size 11°s, 1 orange 7×6mm triangle lampworked bead, 3 size 11°s, 1 light orange 8×15mm glass teardrop, and 4 size 11°s.

Step 5: Thread both ends of the beading wire through 1 red oval 9×4mm glass horizontally drilled oval, 1 teal and gold 15×3mm glass rondelle, 1 frosted clear with orange tips 13×17mm twisted bead, the Fringy Ring, 1 red 6×9mm pressed-glass spiral bead, the Simple Seed Bead Ring made with assorted colors, the Drop Ring made with assorted colors, the crimp tube, 1 gold matte 6×2mm ring, 1 red AB 20×3mm lampworked button with 1 hole, 1 light teal 6×2mm rondelle, and 1 yellow size 8°. Thread the beading wires back through the teal rondelle, the red button, the gold matte 6×2mm ring, and the crimp tube. Crimp the crimp tube and trim the wires close.

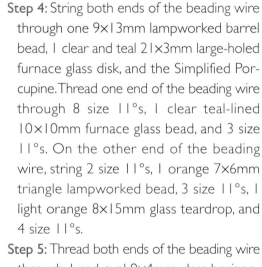

Water Lily Bracelet

Julia Gabriel Robertson

The inspiration for this stunning bracelet was Claude Monet's *Water Lilies,* a painting Julia passed on the way to her office every day when she worked for the Toledo Museum of Art. Although she no longer works at the museum and misses seeing the painting, she now wears a hint of its beauty on her wrist.

Materials
6 g blue AB size 11° Delicas (A)
1 g clear AB size 11° Delicas (B)
44 green white-lined size 11° Japanese seed beads (C)
12 green fire-polished 3mm faceted beads
6 white 7×5mm pressed-glass flower-shaped button beads
1 silver box clasp
1 tension bead
Size D beading thread in color to complement beads

Tools
Size 12 beading needle

Techniques
Tension bead, herringbone stitch

Finished Size
7¼" (18.4 cm)

Step 1: Using 36" (91.5 cm) of thread and leaving an 8" (20.5 cm) tail, string 1 tension bead.
Step 2: String the beads for rows 1 and 2: 1A, *2Cs, and 2As. Repeat from * three

> **TIP** Easy Start
> ✔ Use different colored beads for each of the first three rows of any project worked in herringbone stitch—it will help you visualize which beads will make up these first rows.
> —Meant to Bead

times. String 2Cs and 1A for a total of twenty beads, not counting the tension bead. (Figure 1.)
Step 3: To begin row 3, string 1B and pass back through bead 20. Skip beads 19 and 18, pass back through bead 17, string 2Bs, and pass back through bead 16. Repeat across the row in this manner, skipping 2Cs, passing back through the next A, stringing 2Bs, and passing back through the next A. (Figure 2.)

this project is from

Meant to Bead

**6536 W. Central Ave.
Toledo, OH 43617
(419) 842-8183
meant2bead@aol.com
www.meant2bead.com**

Julia Gabriel Robertson's venture into beading all began with a simple search for the word "beads" on the Internet. After finding an unusual bracelet in an art gallery, she had become fixated on learning the techniques used to create it. Another search for "bead stitching techniques" opened a whole new world, and Meant to Bead was born.

"The idea just clicked," she says. "I had often dreamed of owning my own business, and envisioned the kind of bead store where people could walk in with no knowledge of beading and walk out with something beautiful." Meant to Bead offers 2,000 square feet of a one-stop-shopping experience where customers find glass, semiprecious stone, wood, ceramic, and metal beads, as well as wire, tools, and stringing materials.

Julia's emphasis on new beaders is supported by a wide variety of beading classes and a staff trained to help beginners with stringing and other beading techniques. Worktables are available on a first-come, first-served basis, and a wide selection of beading books and magazines help keep ideas flowing.

And the bracelet that started it all? When Meant to Bead finally opened Julia still didn't know what stitch was used to create that fascinating piece, but one day a teacher brought in her class samples, which included a bracelet made in herringbone stitch—and that's when Julia finally found the technique used to make the inspiring bracelet.

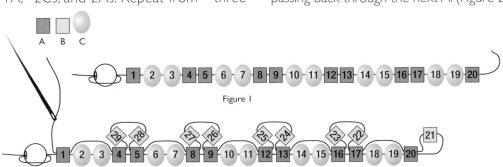

Figure 1

Figure 2

Step 4: Pull on both the tail end and the needle end of the thread to pull the Delicas together. String 1B (bead 30) and 1A (bead 31) and push them down close to the previous row. Pass back through bead 30 (bead 30 is the last bead in row 3 and bead 31 is the first bead in row 4). (Figure 3.)

Step 5: Row 4 is made up of As and is added on top of beads 29 to 21 (Bs) in the following pattern: pass back through bead 29, string 2As, pass through bead 28 and back through 27, string 2As, pass through bead 26 and back through 25. Continue adding As in this manner to end of the row. Always add two more As after going through the last beads in a row, push beads down to the previous row, and pass back through the first of these two new As. (Figure 4.)

Step 6: You should be able to see 10 "columns" of beads forming: the two outside columns stand up, leaning a little to the outside; the other columns lean into each other in pairs forming four "peaks." (Figure 5.)

Step 7: Working with As, continue as in Step 5 for ½" (1.3 cm).

Step 8: *Ripples.* To imitate ripples of water, randomly replace As with Bs anywhere other than the outside columns. Repeat the placement of the As in the same position for several rows to create a short column of the As.

Step 9: *Lily pads and water lilies.* To begin the lily-pad-and-water-lily pattern, *string 1C between the third and fourth beads of a row (Figure 5). Continue across the row as usual. Work back along the next row as usual but pass back through the last C strung and continue the rest of the row as usual. Repeat from *. Begin the next row as usual, but string 1 fire-polished bead above the C. Pass through the fire-polished bead when working back across the next row. Add the flower bead in the same way, but pass through it three times (once as you go across each of the three rows). Continue working rows, reversing the pattern established above (string 1 fire-polished before adding the 2 Cs). You will have completed fifteen rows by the time the lily-pad-and-water-lily pattern is complete. Work 2 rows of As before repeating the lily-pad-and-water-lily pattern, referring to Figure 5.

Step 10: Repeat Step 8 five more times, alternating the lily-pad-and-water-lily pattern between the third and fourth beads and seventh and eighth beads of a row.

Step 12: Remove the tension bead and pass the tail thread through row 1. Use several half hitch knots to secure the thread, weave in the tails, and trim the thread close.

Step 13: Your bracelet is now about 6⅝" (16.8 cm) long. You can alter the length of your bracelet by adding or subtracting lily-pad-and-water-lily pattern repeats; each lily-pad-and-water-lily pattern repeat will add about 1" (2.5 cm).

Step 14: Repeat Step 7.

Step 15: String 1A at the end of the row and 1C. Complete one row using Cs in place of As. Pass back through the row of Cs and pull the ends as in Step 4. Use several half hitch knots to secure the thread, weave in the tails, and trim the thread close.

Step 16: Attach the clasp at both ends, passing the thread through the last rows of As. Use several half hitch knots to secure the thread, weave in the tails, and trim the thread close.

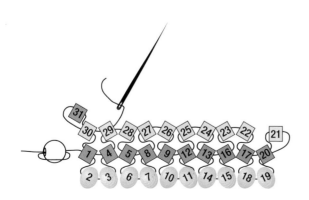

Figure 3

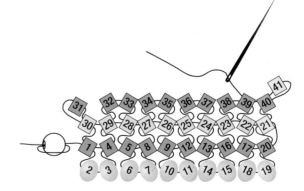

Figure 4

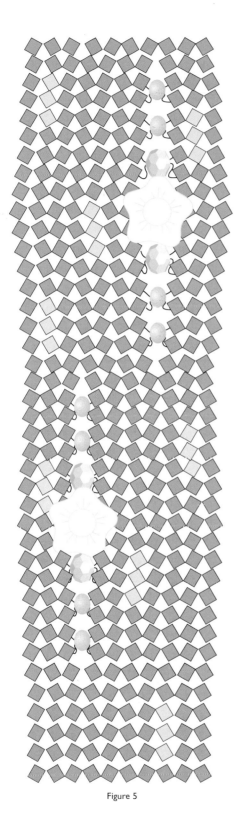

Figure 5

Loopy Ladders

● ● ● ● ● ● ● ● ●

Carolyn Cook and Anne Myserian

Instructor Carolyn and shop owner Anne put their heads together to create this elegant yet funky project made of cube and dagger beads. The base, worked in ladder stitch, gives this necklace a structured feel while the daggers move with the wearer.

Materials
15 g silver-lined amethyst size 11°
 Japanese seed beads
15 g mix of purple matte size 6°
 Czech seed beads
116 amethyst 4×4mm Japanese cube beads
111 amethyst matte AB 5×16mm daggers
1 pewter clasp
Fireline 6 lb test thread

Tools
2 size 12 beading needles
Scissors

Technique
Ladder stitch

Finished Size
19¼" (49 cm)

Step 1: Cut 6' (2 m) of thread and leaving a 5" (12.5 cm) tail, thread a needle on each end. String 1 cube and move to the center of the thread.

Step 2: Using both needles and ladder stitch, join all of the cubes (Figure 1).

Step 3: Turn the work so that the last bead strung is now closest to you. String 8 size 11°s, 1 size 6°, 2 size 11°s, 1 end of the clasp, pass back through the two size 11°s and the size 6°, and string 8 size 11°s (Figure 2). Pass through the loop again to reinforce and tie a surgeon's knot. Glue the knot, hide one thread in the loop, and trim the thread close. Continue working with the remaining needle and thread.

Step 4: *Note:* Keep the needle on top of the beads and do not flip the necklace while working. To begin the loops, bring the thread and needle out of the left side of the second cube (Figure 3).

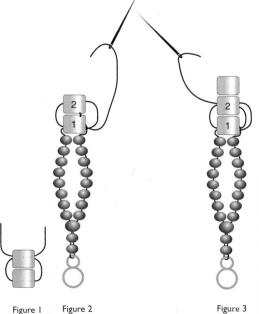

Figure 1   Figure 2   Figure 3

this project is from

Albion Beads

20 Albion St.
Wakefield, MA 01880
(781) 245-1377
albionbeads@aol.com
www.albionbeads.com

Ever attended a bead show? Few words can describe the experience: astonishment, awe, amazement. When customers enter Albion Beads in Wakefield, Massachusetts, owner Anne Myserian wants them to feel just like that. "It's important to me that people be inspired," she says. "I spend a lot of time hand-picking the inventory, and it's exciting to be able to show customers new shapes, colors, and choices."

Large front windows brighten the store and create a perfect spot for customers to attend a beading class or to just pull up a chair to check out the latest bead magazines. Anne prides herself on providing a great variety of silver beads and findings, freshwater pearls, gemstones, Czech pressed-glass flowers and leaves, drops, daggers, dichroic and silver pendants, lampworked beads created by a local artist, and raku pottery beads. Unusual beaded needlework kits, pocketbooks, and scarves are very popular items at Albion Beads. Anne strives to add fresh, unique items every week to keep her regular customers enthused about new projects. Classes on a variety of subjects are offered several times a month, and small group lessons are available for groups of four or more. "Our classes bring a lot of fun into the shop, and the best part is we've all made new beading friends," Anne says.

Step 5: String Pattern A: I size 6°, 4 size 11°s, I dagger, 4 size 11°s, and I size 6°. Skip two cubes and pass through the fifth cube. String Pattern B: 2 size 11°s, I size 6°, and 2 size 11°s. Pass through the sixth cube. (Figure 4.)

Step 6: String Pattern A, pass through the third cube, string Pattern B, and pass through the fourth cube (Figure 5).

Step 7: String Pattern A, pass through the seventh cube, string Pattern B, and pass through the eighth cube (Figure 6).

Step 8: String Pattern C: I size 6°, 4 size 11°s, I dagger, and 4 size 11°s. Pass through both the size 6° to the left of the fifth cube and

the fifth cube. Retrace through the two size 11°s, one size 6°, the two size 11°s that make up Pattern B on the right side of the fifth cube, and pass through the sixth cube and the size 6° on the left of the sixth cube. (Figure 7.)

Step 9: String Pattern D: 4 size 11°s, I dagger, 4 size 11°s, and I size 6°. Pass through the ninth cube, string Pattern B, and pass through the tenth cube. (Figure 8.)

Step 10: Repeat Steps 8–9 until you reach the second-to-last cube.

Step 11: Once you reach the last cube, string the other end of the clasp and end the thread as in Step 3.

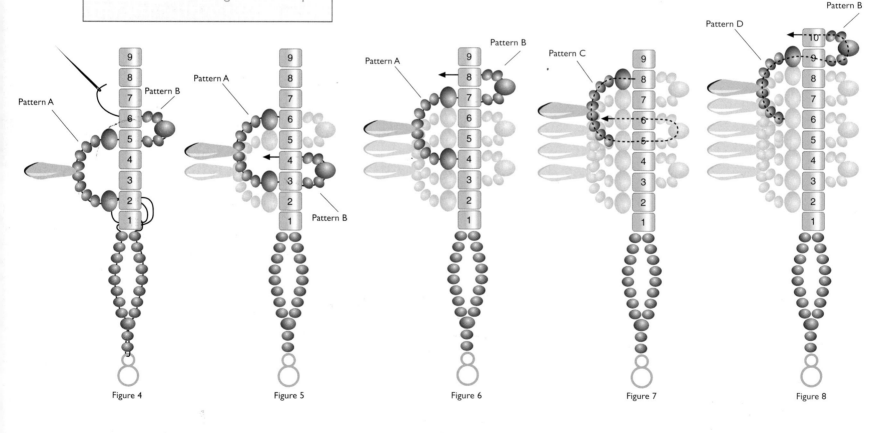

Figure 4　　Figure 5　　Figure 6　　Figure 7　　Figure 8

Crystal Haze
● ● ● ● ● ● ● ● ●

Liz Smith

Liz's necklace is truly a form of fine art. Although the clever use of seed beads and crystals looks challenging, this project can be completed in just a day. The combination of a hammered sterling silver toggle clasp with an assortment of uniquely shaped crystals, silver beads, fringes, and spacers makes for a sparkling necklace that is sure to be noticed.

Materials
15 g silver size 15° Charlottes
144 crystal AB and violet AB 3mm Swarovski crystal bicones
72 light amethyst AB, amethyst AB, and lilac AB 4mm Swarovski crystal bicones
75–100 assorted 3–20mm Swarovski crystals and beads, silver beads, Bali silver spacers, bead caps, and rondelles
1 silver toggle clasp
1 tension bead
Fireline 6 lb test thread

Tools
Size 12 beading needle
Scissors

Techniques
Spiral stitch variation, tension bead, stringing

Finished Size
21" (53.5 cm)

Step 1: *Beadweaving.* *Note:* This stitch is a variation of the basic spiral stitch and has two main parts—the core beads (4mm bicones) and the side beads (5 Charlottes, one 3mm bicone, and 5 Charlottes). If you wish to substitute the size 15° Charlottes with size 13° Charlottes, use four size 13's every place that five size 15's are called for.

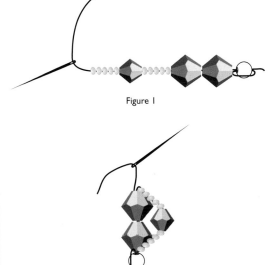

Figure 1

Figure 2

> **TIP** Start with a Long Thread
> ✔ If a design calls for you to work from both directions, begin with an extra long thread: wrap half of it for later and thread your needle on the other end. This eliminates the need for a tension bead and adding a new thread later.
> —The San Gabriel Bead Company

this project is from
The San Gabriel Bead Company

**325 E. Live Oak Ave.
Arcadia, CA 91006
(626) 447-7753
info@beadcompany.com
www.beadcompany.com**

Kelly Thompson, owner of The San Gabriel Bead Company, likes to think of her shop as a "filling station" for beaders. "People come here for good conversation and laughter, to recharge their batteries, to learn something new, for inspiration, and of course to collect bright, shiny objects," she says. "We like to think that our store offers a haven and respite from the craziness of the world around us."

The San Gabriel Bead Company started out as a small shop in 1998, but since then has expanded twice, moving to new locations to accommodate more beads and classroom space. The shop carries a little bit of everything, to please those who like big, bold beads, and those who prefer itty-bitty beads. "Our buyers collect an amazing cornucopia of beads and unique products from all corners of the world, and with these ever-changing treasures we draw an increasing community of people into our store," she says.

Staff members teach an extensive range of workshops, including bead basics, bead stitching, jewelry workshops, introduction to Precious Metal Clay, wire and metal basics, beginning soldering, lampworked beads, and fusing, as well as fine craft workshops on topics including mokume gane beads, stained glass pendants, and mosaic tabletops. Special events include the annual Big Bad Bead Sale, where merchandise is twenty-five percent off the regular price, and trunk shows that feature items that "you cannot live without."

Stop in to share ideas with the talented staff—who are always willing to help begin, finish, or troubleshoot a project—attend a unique workshop or simply unwind after a long day.

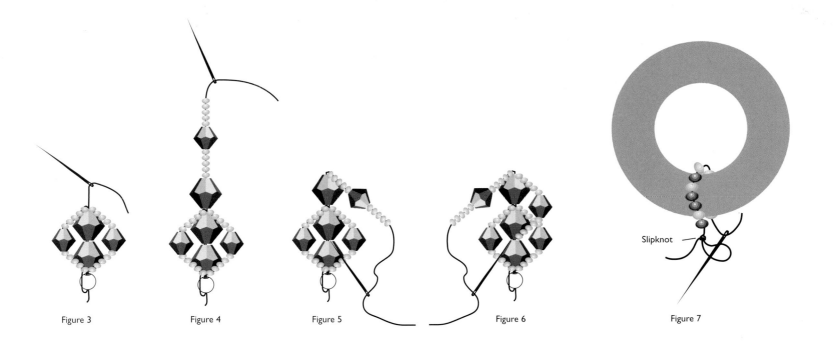

Figure 3   Figure 4   Figure 5   Figure 6   Figure 7

Slipknot

Step 2: String 1 tension bead and 2 core beads. String one set of side beads (Figure 1).

Step 3: Pass through the two core beads (Figure 2).

Step 4: Repeat Step 2 and pass through the two core beads again. Pull the thread tight and flatten the sides so that the thread is centered and exiting out of the top of the top bead. (Figure 3.)

Step 5: String 1 core bead and one set of side beads and slide them down to the other core beads (Figure 4). Pass through the second core bead and the crystal just added (Figure 5). Each new set of side beads will always be on the top of the beads previously strung.

Step 6: String 1 set of side beads and pass the needle through the top two core beads; push the beads to the left side of the core beads (Figure 6).

Step 7: Repeat Steps 5–6 until the piece measures 10¾" (27.5 cm) and the crystals are all used. *Note:* The pattern is established by always picking up a set of side beads and passing through two core beads. After attaching two sets of side beads, step up by adding the core bead called for in Step 5. Be careful to always push the beads to the proper side of the core beads before starting the next loop.

Step 8: *Stringing.* Anchor the thread by weaving the needle through a few of the side and core beads and exit through the last core bead. String assorted beads for 3⅛" (7.8 cm), 7 Charlottes, one end of the clasp, and pass back through the assorted beads. Tie the thread off the with half hitch knots. Repeat on the other end of the beadwoven piece by anchoring the tail of a new thread in the side and core beads before stringing.

Step 9: *Dangles.* Each of the dangles begins as a bead loop that hangs from the clasp and is created independently. The following slipknot method is used to start the dangles: make a slipknot on the end of your thread using a 3" (7.5 cm) tail, keep a finger from your nondominant hand in the knot, and string assorted beads that are no larger than ⅛" (3mm) until you have enough beads to cover the thread when it is looped around the clasp.

Step 10: Insert the needle through the center of the clasp, pass the needle halfway through the slipknot (Figure 7), tighten the slipknot against the needle so the loop in the thread is almost closed, and slowly pull the needle through the slipknot to create the circle of beads around the clasp. Pull the thread to tighten the circle around the clasp, and knot the thread tail and the working thread attached to the needle. Pass the needle through a few beads of the circle to move away from the knot.

Step 11: String 1¾" (4.5 cm) of assorted beads and skipping the last bead strung, pass the needle back through the beads. Make a second pass through the beads around the clasp and down through a few beads in the dangle; reinforce the thread with a few half hitch knots and trim.

Step 12: Repeat Steps 9–11 to create two more dangles.

Femme Fatale Collar

● ● ● ● ● ● ● ● ● ● ● ● ● ●

Kathy Mamat

When Kathy learned basic netting skills from one of her regular customers, Jackie Scieszka, she was immediately addicted to making beaded
collars. The basic netting pattern used in this striking accessory is simple,
so don't be afraid to mix it up: the collar will take on a different personal-
ity—vintage, ethnic, or classic—depending on the type, texture, and color
of beads you choose.

Materials
203 green 4mm freshwater rice pearls
36 green 6mm faceted tourmalated quartz
   round beads
37 green 8mm faceted tourmalated quartz
   round beads
36 green 10×16mm faceted tourmalated
   quartz teardrops
1 Bali silver 12mm round bead
2 Bali silver 6×3mm spacers
36 sterling silver 7×4mm bead caps
Size D beading thread in color to
   complement beads
G-S Hypo Cement

Tools
Size 12 sharps needle

Technique
Netting

Finished Size
14½" (37 cm)

Step 1: Using 6' (2 m) of doubled thread and
leaving a 4" (10 cm) tail, string 2 pearls,
1 spacer, 4 pearls, the 12mm Bali bead,
and 4 pearls. Pass back through the spacer
and first two pearls to form a loop. Tie a
square knot and cement the knot. Let dry
and trim the thread tail close. (Figure 1.)

Figure 1

this project is from

Bead Works Inc.

32751 Franklin Rd.
Franklin, MI 48025
(248) 855-5230
beads@franklinbeadworks.com
www.franklinbeadworks.com

Located in historic Franklin Village in Franklin,
Michigan, Bead Works has been a trendsetter in
the beading community for over twenty-three
years, making it one of the oldest bead shops in
the state. Staffed by experienced bead artists with
an encyclopedic knowledge of design, Bead Works
offers a full range of services, including expert jewelry repair, restringing, and creating magnificent
custom-made jewelry. As manager and buyer,
Kathy Mamat's job is to see that the store is
stocked with an unusual assortment of beautiful
beaded purses, patterns, and vintage jewelry, in
addition to a vast selection of glass and metal
beads and findings.

The shop attracts beaders of all levels; some
live as far away as New York, Miami, and Los Ange-
les, while others are close enough to enjoy the
learning opportunities Bead Works offers. Beaders can schedule private parties, enjoy individual-
ized instruction on a specific project, or master
techniques in classes like basic stringing, beadweaving, peyote stitch, right-angle weave, and Precious
Metal Clay.

"Regardless of the place they call home, all
Bead Works customers share one thing in common—they love the shop's unique combination
of skill and chic," says owner Nomi Joyrich.

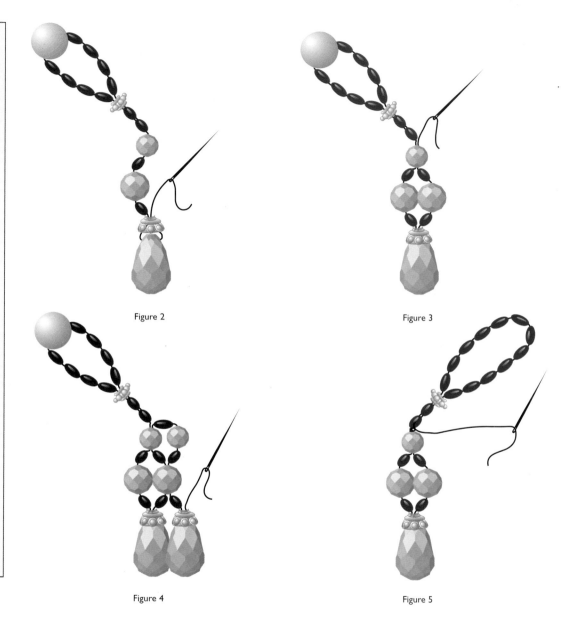

Figure 2

Figure 3

Figure 4

Figure 5

Step 2: String one 6mm quartz, 1 pearl, one 8mm quartz, 1 pearl, 1 cap, and 1 teardrop. Pass back through the cap. (Figure 2.)

Step 3: String 1 pearl, one 8mm quartz, 1 pearl, and pass back through the 6mm quartz added in Step 2 (Figure 3).

Step 4: String 1 pearl, one 6mm quartz, 1 pearl, and pass back through the second 8mm quartz. String 1 pearl, 1 cap, 1 teardrop, and pass back through the cap. (Figure 4.)

Step 5: Repeat Step 3–4 until all of the caps have been added. String 1 pearl, one 8mm quartz, 1 pearl, and pass back through the last 6mm quartz. String 2 pearls, 1 spacer, and 12 pearls. Pass back through the spacer and pearls to form a loop. Tie a square knot and cement the knot. (Figure 5.) Let dry and trim the thread tail close.

Color Play Collage
● ● ● ● ● ● ● ● ● ●

Beverley Smith

Holy Crow Beads owner Beverley Smith loves to weave with beads. In 2004, she was invited to exhibit her work in a show of miniature art, so she created beaded pieces of miniature quilts and this charming beaded sampler. Delicas are perfect for this project, which can be worked in a variety of colorways.

Materials
- 2 g each of black, dark green, gold, lime green, orange, red, turquoise, and white size 11° matte opaque Delicas
- 2 g each of blue, green, red, teal, turquoise, and yellow size 11° Ceylon Delicas
- 2 g each of magenta, purple, and teal size 11° matte translucent Delicas
- 2 g magenta size 11° galvanized Delicas
- 1 piece of 7×7" (18×18 cm) black Ultrasuede or felt

Size D black beading thread
E-6000 Glue

Tools
Twisted wire beading needle
Bead loom
Clear ruler
Scissors

Technique
Loomwork

Finished Size
2⅛×2⅛" (7.3×7.3 cm)

TIPS

Sort Your Beads

✔ Before you start weaving, sort your beads and only use the ones that are the same size. This will help keep the project from distorting.

—Holy Crow Beads

Paint Your Needles

✔ Paint the ends of your flexible wire needles with brightly colored fingernail polish—if you drop a needle, it will be easy to find.

—Bead Bin

Fixing Mistakes

✔ If you make a mistake, don't try to work your needle back through a row. Instead, always remove the needle and gently pull the thread to free the misplaced beads.

—Holy Crow Beads

---

this project is from

Holy Crow Beads

R.R. 1
Clarksburg, ON, Canada N0H 1J0
(519) 599-5697
info@holycrowbeads.com
www.holycrowbeads.com

Head to the hills and leave the pavement behind as you visit Holy Crow Beads in Clarksburg, Ontario, Canada. Located in artist Beverley Smith's studio, this bead shop features a charming woodstove and huge wooden beams, making it the perfect spot to spend an afternoon beading.

Holy Crow opened in 2002, and Beverley has been thrilled with the response to her variety of beads and beading classes. "I've been surprised and delighted to have regular beaders who come once a week. The beading table has brought people together to make incredible creations and incredible friendships," she says.

The shop features hundreds of beads from Japan, the Czech Republic, Austria, Africa, the Middle East, and Bali, all cleverly displayed with art and textiles from those countries. Beaders will also find hundreds of seed beads in various sizes, metal charms, hand-carved bone, Chinese cloisonné, mother-of-pearl, Venetian glass, glass and freshwater pearls, Swarovski crystals, and much more. Findings, tools, and a variety of beading threads and cords are also available, in addition to a library of beading books and a gallery of finished art and jewelry to inspire even the seasoned beader.

"It was trips to Africa that inspired me to work with beads, and now I have found that beading is the perfect marriage of my passions for color, texture, painting, and design," Beverley says. "I love the infinite variety of beads, their combinations, and techniques, as well as the continuous stream of new ideas. I cannot think of anything I'd rather do with my imagination, my hands, and my time . . . except, that is, to share all of this through Holy Crow Beads."

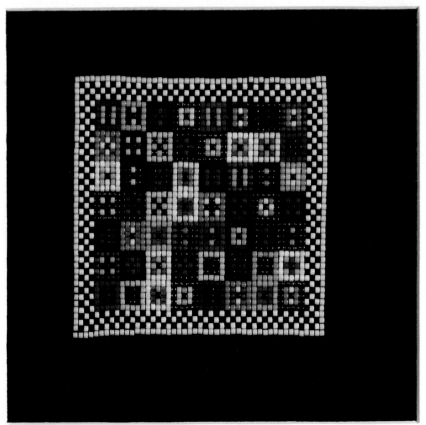

Miniature Quilt Series #8   Beverley Smith '04

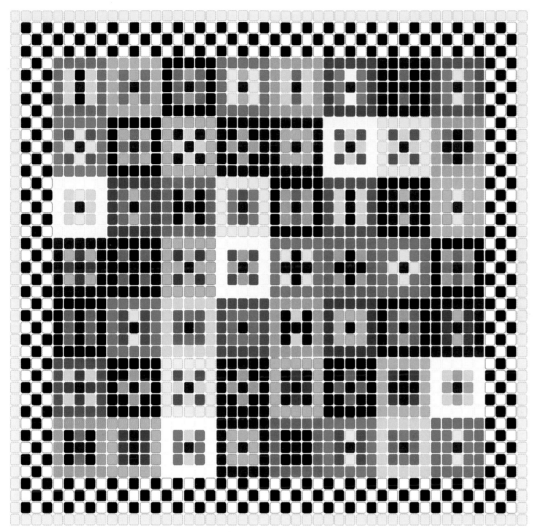

Weaving

Step 1: Use the beading thread and a firm tension to warp the loom. You will need a total of 49 warp threads since the design is 48 beads wide. Be sure the warp threads are centered on the loom for an even tension.

Step 2: To being weaving, thread the needle with 54" (137 cm) of thread for the weft and temporarily tie to the leftmost warp thread, 1" (2.5 cm) above the base of the loom.

Step 3: Following the lowest line of the chart from left to right (Figure 1), string all of the beads for the first row. Gently pulling the thread under the warp threads and using your index finger, push the beads up from beneath the warp threads, distributing the beads so that there is one between each warp thread. Pass the needle back through the row of beads, making sure to pass over the warp threads. *Note:* When adding new threads, leave a 6" (15 cm) tail on both the old thread and on the new thread. Be sure to always start and end threads at the end of rows. If you find that you have too many thread tails to work around, occasionally stop to weave them back into the project.

Step 4: Repeat Step 3, following the remaining 41 rows of the chart.

Finishing

Step 5: Untie the knot created in Step 1 and individually weave each thread tail through several beads; trim the threads close. Leaving about ½" (1.3 cm) tails, cut all of the warp threads. Handle the piece carefully so the beads do not slide loose. Lightly coat the backside of all the beads with glue and place the woven piece, glue side down, on the center of the Ultrasuede or felt and if desired, frame.

☐ White opaque		☐ Turquoise Ceylon	
■ Black opaque		☐ Yellow Ceylon	
☐ Lime green opaque		■ Teal Ceylon	
■ Orange opaque		■ Red Ceylon	
☐ Gold opaque		■ Green Ceylon	
■ Turquoise opaque		■ Blue Ceylon	
■ Red opaque			
■ Dark green opaque		■ Purple matte translucent	
		■ Magenta matte translucent	
■ Magenta galvanized		■ Teal matte translucent	

Stream of Consciousness

● ● ● ● ● ● ● ● ● ● ● ● ● ● ● ● ● ●

Jan Harris, Trish Italia, and Jess Italia

Galena Bead Bar artists Jan, Trish, and Jess put their heads together to create this masterpiece. This breathtaking wire crochet necklace takes you on an artistic journey and dances delicately on chips of turquoise, African opal, labradorite, and pewter butterflies and dragonflies. The project is designed to kindle creativity and intuition for design, and is best suited for advanced beaders.

Materials
16" (40.5-cm) strand turquoise
  6–12mm chips
6 African opal 6–10mm pebbles
6 labradorite 10–14mm pebbles
1 turquoise 20mm nugget
6 pewter 9×8mm butterfly beads
6 pewter 9×6mm dragonfly beads
4 pewter 7×3mm spiral rondelles
8 Bali silver 6×1mm daisy spacers
1 sterling silver 3" (7.5 cm) head pin
2 sterling silver ear wires with balls
1 sterling silver clasp

1 silver 28-gauge 40 yd (37 m) spool
  Artistic wire
E6000 glue

Tools
Wire cutters
Round-nose pliers
Size H/8 (5mm) crochet hook

Techniques
Wire crochet, wireworking, gluing

Finished Size
Necklace 15¾" (40 cm);
  Earrings 2" (5 cm)

TIPS

Relax

✔ If the chains are too tight, simply relax as you pull each stitch through or choose a larger crochet hook. If the chains are too tight, the necklace and earrings will be stiff.

—The Galena Bead Bar

Neat Glue

✔ Use the tip of a needle or toothpick to collect just the right amount of glue—this works great if the tip of the glue container is large and messy.

—Talisman Beads

---

this project is from

The Galena Bead Bar

109 N. Main St.
Galena, IL 61036
(815) 777-4080
galenabeadbar@msn.com
www.galenabeadbar.com

An antique ladder that hangs from the ceiling and is adorned with every color of seed bead is a clue to The Galena Bead Bar's eclectic flair. Throughout the room, tabletop "bars" made from vintage doors and tables spill over with every kind of bead. You'll find beaded art quilts, colorful murals, and wearable art, and music fills the air. When the abundance of color becomes overwhelming, you look up to see a sign that says, "Just Breathe." The Galena Bead Bar has reeled you in!

Founder Jan Harris partnered with mother-and-daughter team Jess and Trish Italia to open the shop, located in the historic Main Street shopping district. Their mission is to guide beaders on an artistic journey, using the array of colors at The Galena Bead Bar to stimulate the senses. The shop is also home to the Bead Divas of Galena, a group of artistic mothers, daughters, and friends.

The Galena Bead Bar truly stands out with unique classes, including stringing and wire crochet. Students can take the Drink and Create workshop, which focuses on incorporating found objects in beadwork; the class begins with a complimentary cappuccino drink whose lid is used to create a pendant for a necklace. At the Picnic in the Park workshop, students enjoy a tasty lunch while working from a fun bracelet kit.

"For decades artists have journeyed to picturesque Galena for inspiration. With the current art and crafts movement that has occurred in Galena, it was just natural that artists filled with passion would unite their talents and create The Galena Bead Bar," Jan says. The shop's motto is truly fitting: "Serving Creativity."

Necklace

Step 1: Set aside 2 spacers, 1 nugget, 1 turquoise chip, 2 butterflies, and 2 spiral rondelles. Roughly lay out the remaining beads in a large circle, equally distributing the silver and stone beads. String the beads on the wire following the random pattern established by the circle.

Step 2: Attach the wire to the crochet hook using a slipknot (Figure 1) and make 3 chains. Bring down a bead and make one chain over the bead (Figure 2). Continue loosely making chains, alternating between some without beads and some with one or two beads, until all the beads are used up and the chain measures about 65" (165 cm).

Step 3: Choosing the sections you like best, cut the strand into three 18" (45.5 cm) strands; reserve two 4" (10 cm) pieces for the earrings. To create a 2" (5 cm) tail for wire wrapping, pull out several stitches and gently pull off the end beads, making sure your beaded area is 14" (35.5 cm) long.

Step 4: Twist together the tail ends of the three wire strands for about 1" (2.5 cm), string one end of the clasp, and make one wrapped loop with all three wires; repeat with the three tails on the other end and the other end of clasp.

Step 5: To make the pendant, string the head pin with 1 spacer, 1 nugget, 1 spacer, 1 turquoise chip, 1 spiral rondelle, and through three crochet stitches, catching the center of each strand; make 1 wrapped loop.

Earrings

Step 1: Cut one 4" (10 cm) piece from the remaining crocheted wire. Fold the piece in half, use both ends to string 1 spiral rondelle, the ear wire, and make a wrapped loop. Wire the butterfly to the base of each earring with a short piece of wire, and glue the wings to one of the turquoise chips.

Step 2: Repeat Step 1 for a second earring.

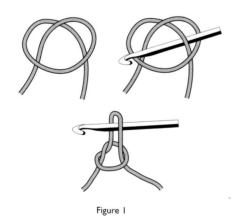

Figure 1

Figure 2

Star Gazing in Santa Fe

Camille Argeanas

Wire joins the dagger beads in this project for a truly original look, while the central crystals glimmer like the stars on a clear Santa Fe night. Camille's simple but elegant project is perfect for new wireworkers who want to try their hand at basic wrapping techniques, and more experienced wireworkers can produce a quick gift.

Materials
- 14 black 5×15mm daggers
- 14 purple 5×15mm daggers
- 16 crystal AB 3mm Czech fire-polished beads
- 16 crystal vitrail 3mm Czech fire-polished beads
- 48" (122 cm) of sterling silver 26-gauge wire
- 2 pairs of sterling silver ear wires

Tools
- Wire cutters
- Flat-nose pliers
- Round-nose pliers

Technique
- Wireworking

Finished Size
- 1⅝" (4.1 cm)

TIP Tuck the Wire Ends
✔ Use the tip of your crimping pliers to tuck sharp, trimmed wire ends into your work.

—Talisman Beads

Black Earrings

Step 1: Cut a 24" (61 cm) piece of wire and string 7 black daggers. Place the beads 6" (15 cm) from one end of the wire

Step 2: Place the beads on a flat surface and form a circle. Cross the ends of the wire over each other to lock the beads in place (Figure 1).

Figure 1

this project is from

Beauty and the Beads Inc.

**939 W. Alameda St.
Santa Fe, NM 87501
(505) 982-5234
beads@santafebeads.com
www.santafebeads.com**

Beaders seeking the unusual and unique will feel right at home at Beauty and the Beads. Located one mile southwest of the Santa Fe Plaza, this welcoming shop fills 800 square feet with a bevy of beads. Owner Madeleine Durham carries an imaginative variety of beads, but says you won't find the shop following national trends or modern fashions. "We focus more on the artistic, diverse, and unique," she says. "We have a lot of artistic people here, so we carry everything from the basic to the eclectic." She recently added a line of belly dance jewelry for Santa Fe's many belly dancers.

Madeleine opened the store in 1991 when her fledgling bead business—which started out in a Santa Fe flea market—began growing faster than she expected. "People often comment on how wonderful the feeling is in our store," Madeleine says. "Everyone on our team is a creative problem solver and we enjoy helping customers with their projects."

The store supplies basic tools and findings as well as seed beads, semiprecious stones, crystals, metal beads, pendants, charms, original art beads, and bone and clay beads. "We try to make the shop very user friendly, so people can touch and feel everything," Madeleine says. "It's the kind of shop that when people come in, they immediately feel comfortable." Professional teachers offer classes and workshops on a variety of topics, including basic stringing, wirework, and seed bead stitching.

Step 3: Hold the beads between two fingers to keep them flat. Begin to weave over and under each petal with the longest end of the wire, making sure to stay close to the center. Continue weaving until you have three wraps on top of each petal. (Figure 2.)

Step 4: Randomly switch between the AB fire-polished and vitrail fire-polished beads as you work: *string 2 beads on one of the wires, fold the wire over the center of the flower, and string 2 more beads before pulling the wire across the back. Pull the wire across the back and bring it to the front between two different daggers. Repeat from * so that there are four beads on each side. Finish by tucking the wire between two beads and trim the wire close. (Figure 3.)

Step 5: Join the flower to one ear wire by making a small wrapped loop with the wire not used for wrapping and trim the wire close (Figure 4).

Step 6: Repeat Steps 1–5 for a second earring.

Purple Earrings

Step 7: Repeat Steps 1–6 using the purple daggers in place of the black daggers for a second pair of earrings.

Figure 2

Figure 3

Figure 4

this project is from

Sorrelli

45 S. Main St.
Sheridan, WY 82801
(307) 673-0844
lori@labeadsorrelli.com
www.labeadsorrelli.com

At the base of the Big Horn Mountains in Sheridan, Wyoming, shoppers can find a little bead shop with a great big heart. Sorrelli, operated by Lori Kindle, cultivates a cozy, friendly atmosphere for beaders and knitters to shop, learn, browse, and share ideas. "We feel that we don't have customers, but beading and knitting friends," she says.

Lori opened the shop in 2003, shortly after moving to Sheridan and realizing that the closest bead store was 120 miles away. In addition to the standard bead shop inventory, Sorrelli carries an array of yarn and notions for knitting and felting and specializes in one-of-a-kind beaded handbags.

The shop features beads from around the world, including glass, cloisonné, bone, lampworked, Bali silver, vermeil, gold-filled, pewter, bugle, and cylinder beads, as well as Swarovski crystals in more than 100 colors, sterling silver findings, and Czech and Japanese seed beads. Lori stocks a selection of books and magazines, quality beading tools, needles, and containers for bead storage. In addition to teaching classes and offering minor jewelry repair and restringing, she also executes custom work in fine silver, ranging from complete necklaces and earrings to simple charms.

Lori says she loves the shop because it connects her with a network of beading and knitting friends. "Almost everyday someone tells us that they are so happy we opened our little store. You'll always find a new beader looking over the shoulder of an experienced beader, looking to find something new and interesting."

Gold Pearl Goddess Earrings

Jaci Kindle

These earrings, created by Lori's twenty-five-year-old daughter, are a new interpretation of the popular chandelier earring. Shiny pearls paired with gold chain make these earrings fit for any goddess. For an interesting variation, try combining sterling silver chain with cube pearls.

> **TIP** Enlarge Holes in Beads
> ✔ Use a Dremel tool with a fine-grit tip to enlarge holes in glass, resin, and many clay beads and pearls: place them in a shallow bowl with water and carefully drill away.
> —Bead Dreams

Materials
- 2 peach 12mm freshwater pearl coins
- 1 pair of gold-filled earring studs with loops
- 15½" (39.5 cm) of gold-filled small (1.5×2mm links) chain
- 7" (18 cm) of gold-filled 20-gauge wire

Tools
- Round-nose pliers
- Wire cutters

Technique
- Wireworking

Finished Size
- 2" (5 cm)

Step 1: Cut the chain into four ½" (1.3 cm) pieces, two 1¾" (4.5 cm) pieces, two 2¼" (5.5 cm) pieces, and two 2¾" (7 cm) pieces. Cut the gold wire into two 3½" (9 cm) pieces.

Step 2: Make a wrapped loop on one end of one 3½" (9 cm) piece of wire, enclosing the following in the loop: one end of one ½" (1.3 cm) piece of chain, one end of one 2¾" (7 cm) piece of chain, one end of one 2¼" (5.5 cm) piece of chain, and one end of one 1¾" (4.5 cm) piece of chain (Figure 1).

Step 3: Wrap the wire to close the loop.

Step 4: String 1 pearl on the wire and make a wrapped loop on the other end of the wire, enclosing the ends of the 1¾" (4.5 cm),

2¼" (5.5 cm), and 2¾" (7 cm) pieces of wire previously strung, and a second ½" (1.3 cm) piece of chain in the loop (Figure 2).

Step 5: Wrap the wire to close the loop (Figure 3).

Step 6: Open the loop on one earring stud, string the loose ends of both ½" (1.3 cm) pieces of chain, and close the earring stud loop.

Step 7: Repeat Steps 1–6 for a second earring.

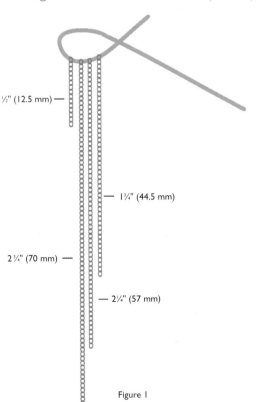

½" (12.5 mm) —

— 1¾" (44.5 mm)

2¾" (70 mm) —

— 2¼" (57 mm)

Figure 1

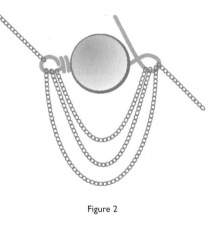

Figure 2

Figure 3

Retro Rosette Brooch

● ● ● ● ● ● ● ● ● ● ● ● ● ● ● ●

Katherine Robinson

Katherine's colorful brooch, with a central group of teardrop beads on a bed of seed beads, features a striking color palette of vintage-feeling brown, gold, and turquoise. The picot edges add a three-dimensional flair, dressing up a cardigan sweater or your favorite coat. Katherine thanks Cynthia Rutledge for instructing her how to add the herringbone-stitch embellishment.

Materials
5 g light teal size 15° Japanese seed beads
10 g green matte size 15° Japanese seed beads
10 g light green translucent size 15° Japanese seed beads
10 g light teal size 11° Japanese seed beads
10 g dark gold size 11° Japanese seed beads
5 g light gold size 11° galvanized Japanese seed beads
23 peridot AB 4mm Swarovski crystal bicones
1 light topaz 6mm Swarovski crystal bicone
6 turquoise 12×8mm vertically drilled teardrops
1 gold-filled 1½" (3.8 cm) pin back
1 white 2½" (6.5 cm) circle of Lacy's Stiff Stuff
1 dark teal 2" (5 cm) circle of leather
Size D beading thread in color to complement beads
G-S Hypo Cement

Tools
2 size 12 beading needles
Toothpick

Techniques
Herringbone stitch, peyote stitch, bead embroidery

Finished Size
2½" (6.5 cm) in diameter

TIPS

The Perfect Color
✔ When designing an accessory for a friend, be sure to add their eye color to the design—this will guarantee that the colors will look great on them.
—The Bead Shop

Slow Down
✔ "Beading is not a speed sport." Remember that beading is not a race—sit back and enjoy the process.
—Creative Castle

---

this project is from

Beads by Design

585 Cobb Pkwy. S., Ste. L
Marietta, GA 30060
(770) 425-3909

Beads by Design, which started as a jewelry gallery more than eight years ago, has evolved into a thriving bead shop and artistic meeting place. Owner Gerry White, a German-trained goldsmith, transformed the original gallery into a jewelry supply store after discovering that customers wanted to create jewelry of their own.

Located in the Artisan Resource Center in a beautiful suburb of Atlanta, Beads by Design now offers 2,500 square feet of beads, jewelry, and classroom space. The shop has soaring eighteen-foot (5.5 m) high ceilings, plenty of display space, and features an ever-growing selection of vintage and contemporary beads from around the world, including Czech fire-polished beads, Austrian crystals, Japanese seed beads, Delicas, precious metals, books, and tools.

Over the years the shop has become a gathering place for the crafting community. Beads by Design participates in a yearly open house to introduce customers to glass blowers, sculptors, glass beadmakers, portrait artists, woodworkers, and other artists in the community. The Southern Flames, a local chapter of The International Society of Glass Beadmakers, meets regularly at the shop and hosts special glass beadmaking classes. Students can choose from a variety of other classes, too, including jewelry making, stringing, loomwork, pearl knotting, Precious Metal Clay, wireworking, fusing, macramé, amulet bags, and embroidered bags. A team of eight instructors continually stretch their imaginations for new class ideas.

"Our goal has been to provide unique and original beads and a variety of classes," Gerry says. "We cater to all skill levels, and encourage our students to design and create on their own."

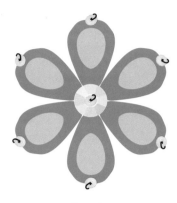

Figure 1

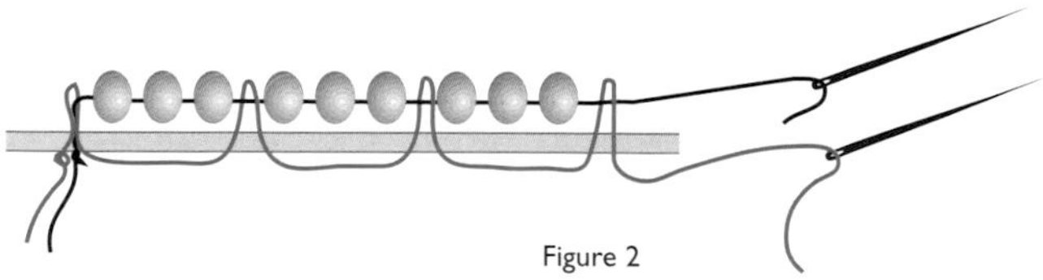

Figure 2

Step 1: Bring the needle up in the center of the Stiff Stuff, string one 6mm bicone, 1 galvanized size 11°, and pass back through the 6mm bicone and the Stiff Stuff. *Bring the needle up about ⅛" (3mm) away and string 1 teardrop bead, 1 galvanized size 11°, pass back through the teardrop and the Stiff Stuff, bring the needle up at the tip of the teardrop bead, pass through the teardrop, and take the needle down in the center to anchor the teardrop. Repeat from * five times to form a cluster. (Figure 1.)

Step 2: Bring the needle up along the outside edge of a teardrop and string 1 galvanized size 11°, one 4mm bicone, and 1 galvanized size 11°. Lay the beads flat on the surface of the Stiff Stuff along the edge of a teardrop, and take the needle down after the last strung bead. Anchor the beads with backstitch: bring the needle up between the first size 11° and the crystal, and pass back through the 4mm bicone and the galvanized size 11°. Continue in this manner until all the teardrops are surrounded.

Step 3: Working from the inside out and following the contours of the beads added in Step 2, couch down one row each of light green size 15°s, green matte size 15°s, light teal size 11°s, and three rows of dark gold size 11°s (Figure 2).

Step 4: Working with dark gold size 11°s, create the ruffle along the outside edge of the Stiff Stuff: using the last row stitched in Step 3 as the base, work four rows of peyote stitch. Create the picot edge on the ruffle with light teal size 11°s, working the thread up from the bottom of the Stiff Stuff to anywhere along the top of the peyote rim: *string 3 light teal size 15°s and pass through the next dark gold size 11°. Repeat from * until you reach the starting point. Weave the thread down to the base of the Stiff Stuff.

Step 5: Center the pin back on the right side of the leather. Mark the location of the hinge and fastener and make two parallel vertical slits in the leather and one horizontal slit that connects the top ends of the two vertical slits. Slide the leather flap created by the slits through the pin back, making sure that the pin is on top. Using a toothpick, evenly apply a small amount of cement to the wrong side of the Stiff Stuff and press to the wrong side of the leather, enclosing the base of the pin back. Allow to dry for at least three hours.

Step 6: Using dark gold size 11°s, work one row of brick stitch and then two rows of herringbone stitch around the base on the edge of the leather. To begin working brick stitch, string 2 beads and insert the needle into the leather from the right side to the wrong side of the leather. Bring the needle up about two bead's width away from the thread, move the needle up through the beads in the direction you want to stitch. Take the needle down into the first bead and up through the second bead. From this point forward, string one bead at a time and stitch into the leather from the right side to the wrong side, a bead's width away from where you started; bring the needle back up through the last bead added. Continue in this manner all the way around and anchor the needle and thread into the first bead on the completed row. To begin working herringbone stitch, *place two beads on the needle, take the needle down into the next edge bead, and

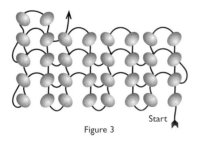

Figure 3

Start

bring the needle up into the next edge bead. Repeat from * until you reach the end of the row. Work one row and anchor the needle and thread into the first bead of the row; if you are left with a single bead to work your last stitch in, instead of threading a pair of beads, thread two beads on the needle and take the needle back down into the bead that the thread is exiting out of. Complete the row with a step up. Work one more row of herringbone stitch around. (Figure 3.)

Step 7: To work picots on the last row of herringbone stitches, the thread should be exiting out of the rightmost bead of a herringbone pair. *String 3 light teal size 15°s and take the needle down in the next bead. Bring the needle up through the first bead of the next pair. Repeat from * until you reach the beginning of the row. Weave your thread down to the base of the pin.

Step 8: Couch down one row of dark gold size 11°s between the base row of picots and ruffle created in Step 4 along the outside edge of the pin. Weave your thread down to the back of the Stiff Stuff, knot the thread, and trim the thread close.

Venetian Zing Ring

Stacy Broas

Ancient Roman designs inspired Stacy to create this eye-catching ring. Drawing on her knowledge of macramé, she cleverly created the wire equivalent of a lark's head knot, resulting in a custom-fitting ring. Although any large-holed bead could be used in this design, this gleaming Venetian glass bead gives it extra zing.

Materials
1 green foil 12×12×6mm Venetian glass
  square bead
12" (30.5 cm) of sterling silver 18-gauge
  half-hard wire

Tools
Round-nose pliers
Chain-nose pliers

Wire cutters
Ring mandrel
Ring sizer
Rubber or rawhide mallet

Technique
Wireworking

Finished Size
1" (2.5 cm) tall

TIPS

Use Large Wire

✔ Most holes in beads will accommodate size 20-gauge wire. However, the ring in this project will be stronger and hold its round shape better if you stick to using 18-gauge half-hard wire, making it worth the time spent looking for a large-holed bead.

Omit the Spirals

✔ Although rare, the spirals on the ring in this project can catch on your clothing. If you are afraid of hooking the spirals, just trim the wires close in Steps 5 and 6 instead of making spirals.

—The Creative Fringe

---

this project is from
The Creative Fringe LLC

210 Washington Ave.
Grand Haven, MI 49417
(616) 296-0020
stacy@thecreativefringe.com
www.thecreativefringe.com

If you dream about beads, be sure to visit The Creative Fringe for an experience in beading bliss. "My goal is to create utopia for beaders and jewelry designers, and to teach others the joy of making things with their own hands," says proprietor Stacy Broas, who opened the shop in 2003 after spending many years in the field of textiles.

Located on Grand Haven's main street, the shop exudes a feeling of serenity and tranquility. Colorful beads beckon from the front window, while local art and paper lanterns decorate the walls and high ceilings. You'll find an extensive collection of well-organized beads, findings, tools, books, glass lampworking supplies, wire, and sheet metal, as well as a staff that specializes in jump-starting your creativity. The shop's class roster includes basic stringing, beginning wire wrapping, Precious Metal Clay basics, beginning peyote stitch, knotting, and advanced classes that focus on metalworking techniques.

Events like "Bring Your Own Bead" night, designed specifically for beaders to complete their UFOs (unfinished objects) or to begin new ones, along with bead parties and regular beading demonstrations, round out the shop's busy schedule. Beaders are always welcome to pull up a chair at a workstation and work on projects during regular business hours.

Stacy continually strives to provide a fulfilling experience for every beader who visits The Creative Fringe. "We may not have reached total utopian status yet," she says "but we are getting closer every day."

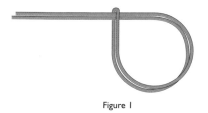

Figure 1

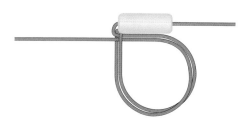

Figure 2

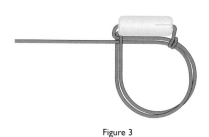

Figure 3

Step 1: Bend the piece of wire in half around the tip of the round-nose pliers to create a rounded bend in the wire.

Step 2: Determine the size you want your ring to be and add about a ¼ of a size. Hold the wire between the thumb and fingers of your nondominant hand about ½" (1.3 cm) below the bend. Bring both ends of the wire through the loop formed by the bend created in Step 1 and pull the ends until a circle shape is formed loosely around your thumb (Figure 1).

Step 3: Transfer the circle of wire to the ring mandrel. Continue to pull the ends of the wire through the loop until you have the size you need, starting small and then pushing the ring down to the correct size. Watch to make sure the wires remain parallel and do not cross each other. If needed, round the shape of the wire with the mallet.

Step 4: Remove the ring from the mandrel. Grab one of the wires and bend it down across the top of the ring. Thread the bead onto this wire and push the bead up against the bend; there will be a little bit of space between the bend and the bead (Figure 2).

Step 5: Wrap the wire that exits the bead around the side of the ring, making about 2½ wraps (Figure 3). Trim the wire to ¾" (2 cm) long, make a spiral using the chain-nose pliers, and press it against the side of the bead (Figure 4).

Step 6: Wrap the remaining length of wire around the upwrapped side of the ring at the end of the bead 2½ times. Trim the wire to 1" (2.5 cm) and make a spiral using the chain-nose pliers, leaving enough space at the base to bend the wire over the top of the bead; bend the spiral down to the surface of the bead (Figure 5).

Step 7: Return the ring to the ring mandrel and hammer around the base of the ring until the ring is round again, being careful not to hit the bead. (Excessive pounding can result in a ring that is too large.)

Side view

Figure 4

Top view

Figure 5

Dancing Dragonfly

Nadia Wilson

Accessorize your favorite jacket, sweater, or handbag with Nadia's sweet pin. Not only are the ladder-stitch wings fun to make, they're surprisingly quick to complete. For a little extra color and pizzazz in your home, omit the pin back, attach the dragonfly to a length of wire, and stand the "insect" in the base of your favorite houseplant.

Materials
- 12 g silver-lined peach AB size 11° Japanese seed beads
- 5 hematite size 8° Japanese seed beads
- 7 hematite size 6° Japanese seed beads
- 1 crystal AB fire-polished 8mm Czech faceted rondelle
- 7 crystal fire-polished 6mm Czech faceted rounds
- 2 crystal AB fire-polished 8mm faceted teardrops
- 1" (2.5 cm) long pin back with three holes
- 24" (61 cm) of 24-gauge beading wire
- 10' (3 m) of 28-gauge beading wire

Tools
- Round-nose pliers
- Chain-nose pliers
- Wire cutters

Techniques
- Ladder stitch, stringing

Finished Size
3¼×4¼" (8.5×11 cm)

Step 1: *Body.* Cut a 15" (38 cm) piece of 24-gauge wire, string 1 size 8°, and bring the bead to the center of the wire. Bring the two wire ends together and string both ends through one 6mm round. Add 1 size 6° and

> **TIP** Clean Crystals
> ✔ Use this rule of thumb for jewelry made with Swarovski crystals: last thing on, first thing off. This way the crystals stay shiny, free of makeup and hairspray.
>
> —Urban Girl

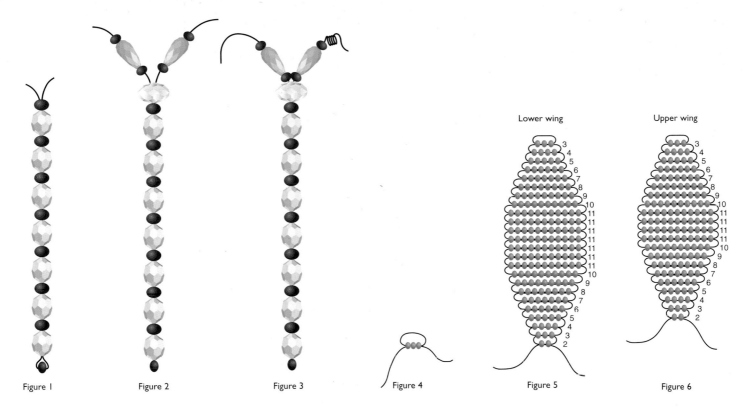

Lower wing	Upper wing

Figure 1 Figure 2 Figure 3 Figure 4 Figure 5 Figure 6

one 6mm round. Continue adding beads in this pattern until you have added all seven 6mm rounds, ending with a size 6°. (Figure 1.) String the 8mm round for the head and separate the wires. On each wire, string 1 size 8°, a faceted teardrop (insert the wire into the narrow end first), and one size 8° (Figure 2). Coil each wire end with the round-nose pliers to make about five spirals. Trim the wire ends close and push the spiral down against the beads (Figure 3).

Step 2: *Lower wings.* Cut a 30" (76 cm) piece of 28-gauge wire. To work row 1, string 3 size 11°s and bring them to the center of the wire, take one end of the wire and pass through all three beads again, and pull tight, maintaining gentle tension to avoid kinks in the wire (Figure 4). To work row 2, string 4 size 11°s on one wire end, slide them down to the previous row, pass the other wire end back through them, and pull both wire ends

tight. Referring to Figure 5 (the numbers on the illustration indicate the number of beads in each row), continue adding rows of size 11°s in this manner, increasing until there are eleven beads in a row and then reduce rows back down to two beads; the number of beads in each row is as follows: row 3=5 beads, row 4=6 beads, row 5=7 beads, row 6=8 beads, row 7=9 beads, row 8=10 beads, row 9=11 beads, row 10=11 beads, row 11=11 beads, row 12=11 beads, row 13=11 beads, row 14=11 beads, row 15=11 beads, row 16 =10 beads, row 17=9 beads, row 18=8 beads, row 19=7 beads, row 20=6 beads, row 21=5 beads, row 22=4 beads, row 23=3 beads, and row 24=2 beads. Twist the two wires together gently with needle-nose pliers after the last row. Repeat for a second lower wing. (Figure 5.)

Step 3: *Upper wings.* Repeat as in Step 2, the number of beads in each row is as follows-

row 1=3 beads, row 2=4 beads, row 3=5 beads; row 4=6 beads, row 5=7 beads, row 6=8 beads, row 7=9 beads, row 8=10 beads, row 9=11 beads, row 10=11 beads, row 11=11 beads, row 12=11 beads, row 13=10 beads, row 14=9 beads, row 15=8 beads, row 16=7 beads, row 17=6 beads, row 18=5 beads, row 19=4 beads, row 20=3 beads, row 21=2 beads. Repeat for a second upper wing. (Figure 6.)

Step 4: *Attach the wings.* The top wings are attached in between the uppermost 6mm round and the size 6° above it. Twist the wing wires in between these two beads a couple of times. Attach the bottom wings the same way, but place them between the next 6mm down and the size 6° above it. Bring the wires to the back, insert through the holes in the pin back, twist together, and trim the wires close. Adjust the body so that it has a gentle curve.

Doorway Dangles

Genelle Peterson

Genelle's stunning curtain, suitable for any doorway, window, or wall, incorporates many types of beads into a cohesive work of art. If you aren't in need of a curtain, use sparkling crystals and seed beads to create individual short strands that can be used as "icicles" for holiday decoration. Using a Beadspinner, these beautiful beaded strands are fast and easy to make.

Materials
- 300–350 g assorted black size 5–10° rocailles, square beads, and Japanese seed beads
- 500–600 assorted black and hematite 4–11mm Swarovski crystal cubes, bicones, teardrops, flat rounds, faceted rounds, bicones, and barrels
- 50–60 assorted 10–56mm lampworked, furnace, metal, and semiprecious beads
- 190 sterling silver 1×2mm crimp tubes
- 150–160' (46–49 m) of .010 beading wire
- Clear tape
- 1 black 22½" (57 cm) long curtain rod with mounting hooks

Tools
- Beadspinner
- Hooked needle (2 included with spinner)
- Needle-nose pliers
- Crimping pliers
- Wire cutters

Technique
- Stringing

Finished Size
- 20" (51 cm), longest strand

Note: Several of the lampworked beads are available from Frantz Art Glass and Suppliers Inc.; (360) 427-6572; pat@patfrantzstudio.com; www.patfrantzstudio.com. If you are unable to find the beads used in this project, choose favorite beads from your stash, including antique and lampworked beads.

TIPS

Use Wire
✔ Although it is easier to use the Beadspinner with thread than wire, it's best to use .010 beading wire for the beaded curtain because of the wire's strength and its reluctance to tangle.

Control Your Speed
✔ The size of bead picked up by the Beadspinner will depend on the speed of the spin and the placement of the needle. Generally a slower speed will allow the needle hook to pick up larger beads, while a faster speed will pick up smaller beads. Placing the hook higher along the side of bead bowl will also encourage the hook to pick up larger beads.

—International Glass & Bead Company

this project is from

International Glass & Bead Company

317 W. First St.
Claremont, CA 91711
(909) 626-0877
info@glassandbeads.com
www.glassandbeads.com

You may notice a subtle, yet energetic buzz as you enter the front door of International Glass & Bead Company. Owner Genelle Peterson says that's the sound of beaders hanging out in the shop, shopping, designing jewelry, and passing along their experience to others. "Since day one twenty years ago, hands-on instruction has been our focus," says Genelle. Her love for "sharing knowledge with the newcomers" adds to the friendly atmosphere.

International Glass & Bead Company sells fine crystal and art glass, but the main attraction for beaders is the "bead room." Separate from the crystals and glass displays, the bead room features glass beads, finished jewelry, fine clasps, an array of Swarovski beads and prisms, gemstones, trade beads, Czech beads, Japanese seed beads, and more. "From the start our customers wanted more, so we just keep adding," says Genelle.

In addition to the vast selection of beads, you'll also find all the stringing supplies, findings, and books and magazines needed to create fabulous jewelry and accessories. The store recently added a "crystal embellishment" department that features iron-on crystals, sew-ons, and prisms. Genelle says this new addition helps satisfy her customers looking to spice up their home décor, fiber arts, quilts, fabric dolls, and clothing. She loves to see her customers stretch their creativity and always strives to provide a creative, inspiring environment.

Figure 1   Figure 2

Step 1: Fill half of the bowl of the Beadspinner with beads. Cut the wire into ninety-five 15–23" (38–58.5 cm) pieces.

Step 2: To make the bottom loop: thread the needle of the Beadspinner with one of the pieces of cut wire, leaving a 1" (2.5 cm) tail. Use the Beadspinner to fill the needle with 7–8 size 5–10°s, push beads from the needle onto one strand, string 1 of the large beads, 7–8 size 5–10°s, and 1 crimp tube. Insert the tail into the crimp tube and crimp; trim the tail wire close. (Figure 1.) Bottom loops can also be made by stringing a crimp tube and a teardrop bead, threading the wire back through the crimp tube, and crimping; trim the tail wire close (Figure 2).

Step 3: Use the Beadspinner to string about 12–20" (30.5–51 cm) of beads, leaving about 3" (7.5 cm) of bare wire and taping the end of the strand.

Step 4: To make the top loop: string 1 crimp tube and 3" (7.5 cm) of size 5–10°s. Insert the end of wire into crimp tube and crimp; trim the excess wire close.

Step 5: Repeat Steps 2–4 for the remaining strands, using both methods of creating the bottom loops from Step 2.

Step 6: Mount the curtain rod hooks to a wall or in a doorway or window. String the curtain rod through the top loops of the strands and mount the rod on the hooks.

> **VARIATION** To make icicles (individual strands) to garnish your house plants, windows, or holiday tree: string 1 crimp tube, 1 white or clear teardrop or Swarovski crystal pendant with a bead cap, pass the end of the wire back though the crimp tube and crimp; trim the wire close. String assorted silver-lined crystal beads, clear crystal Swarovski, fire-polished glass beads, and clear, white, gray, red, and metal seed beads for 13½–20½" (34.5–52 cm), beginning and ending the strand with 3–5 larger beads. Finish the end as when beginning the wire.

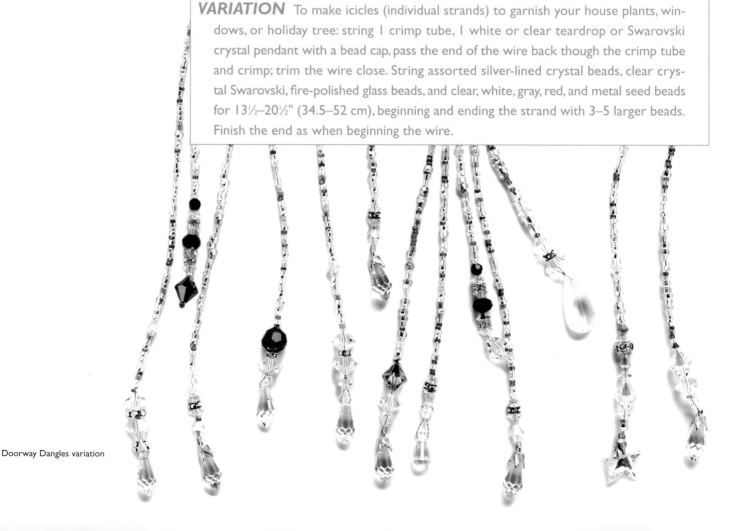

Doorway Dangles variation

Let's Play Tic-Tac-Toe

Betsy Perdue

Tic-tac-toe brings back fond childhood memories, and in this project Betsy turns striking ceramic buttons into game pieces, incorporating simple bead-embroidery techniques in a functional design. Make and embellish a pouch for storing these unique game pieces and learn to add just the amount of fringe you want. It's not often that you'll find a game made from beads and buttons!

Materials

- 60 g red size 11° Czech seed beads
- 5 g black size 8° Czech seed beads
- 5 red and black 23×32mm oval ceramic buttons
- 5 red and black 30×30mm ceramic buttons
- 1 sterling silver 34×32mm tic-tac-toe charm
- 1 sterling silver 7mm jump ring
- 1 piece 8¾× 8¾" (22×22 cm), 1 piece 9½×4" (24×10 cm), 5 pieces 1×1" (2.5×2.5 cm), and 5 oval pieces 1¼×¾" (3.2×2 cm) of black Ultrasuede
- Size D beading thread in color to complement fabric
- 5" (12.5 cm) of copper 18-gauge wire
- E6000 glue
- 1 wood block 10½×10½×¾" (26.5×26.5×2 cm) with feet
- Double-stick tape

Tools

- Size 10 beading needle
- Dressmaker's white chalk

Techniques

Bead embroidery, fringing, gluing

Finished Size

11×¾×11¾" (30×30 cm) board, 3½×4½" (9×11.5 cm) closed pouch

> **TIP** More Fringe
> ✔ For a fuller look, make more passes of "frothy fringe" in Steps 3, 7, and 11.
> —Beads & Beyond

Board

Step 1: Use the chalk to lightly mark the tic-tac-toe grid on the 8¾×8¾" (22×22 cm) piece of Ultrasuede.

Step 2: Using size 8°s and backstitch with beads, stitch lines that are about 2" (5 cm) long and cover the chalk lines; do not stitch where the chalk lines of the board intersect. Using a single knotted thread, bring the needle up from the back to begin working beaded backstitch: Pick up 3 beads, *slide the beads down, lay them down on the Ultrasuede along the line, and pass the needle through the Ultrasuede at the edge of

this project is from

Beads & Beyond

25 102nd Ave. NE
Bellevue, WA 98004
(425) 462-8992

For Kathy Dannerbeck, co-owner of Beads & Beyond in Bellevue, Washington, opening a bead store was a "no brainer." After owning a weaving, craft, and beading studio for many years, she realized that beads were "slowly taking over." She decided to throw her energies behind the beading movement and enjoy the ride.

In 1994, Kathy and her husband, Peter, opened a full-service bead store with an extensive supply of beads and buttons. Two years later, they created an exclusive line of glass buttons manufactured in the Czech Republic, which they now sell to bead, fabric, and fiber arts stores across the country.

You can't help feeling drawn to the beads when you walk into Beads & Beyond. Cupboards, drawers, and shelves are filled with every sort of bead imaginable, including Czech lampworked beads, an overwhelming inventory of buttons, Swarovski crystals, a wide selection of silver beads and findings, pearls, and 2,000 types of seed beads. Kathy says she believes there's enough extra inventory in the shop to open a whole new bead store. Although Kathy would love to add additional space for new products—like fibers, which are emerging in the beading world—she doesn't want the shop to lose its cozy feel. Customers are welcome to relax on the couch and read books or magazines, and a kid's room provides a special place for the younger crowd.

Beads & Beyond offers more than 100 class sessions in a four-month period on a variety of subjects including stringing, off-loom beading techniques, wirework, and Precious Metal Clay. The staff of twenty-five is always introducing something exciting. "We strive to challenge and inspire our customers," Kathy says, "and we appreciate the opportunity to share with others."

Frothy fringe

Figure 1

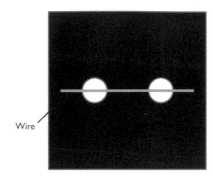

Wire

Figure 2

Button

Wire   Base

Figure 3

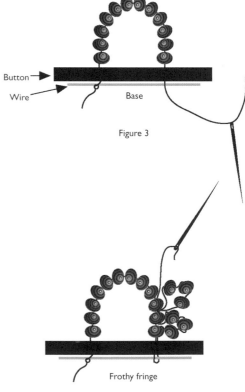

Frothy fringe

Figure 4

the last bead strung. Bring the needle up between the first and second beads strung, pass through the second and third beads strung, pick up 3 beads, and continue from * to the end of the row. Bead embroider all the grid lines in the same manner to create the base for the "frothy fringe."

Step 3: To cover the size 8°s with "frothy fringe," bring the needle up at the end of one base row of size 8°s, *string 3 size 11°s, and pass through the next size 8°. Repeat from * until the base row is covered. (Figure 1.) After exiting the last bead in the base row, string 3 size 11°s and bring the needle to the back of the Ultrasuede, making a picot at the end of the row. Reverse direction and repeat.

Step 4: Repeat Step 3 to embellish all of the backstitched lines created in Step 2.

Step 5: Adhere the Ultrasuede to the base using the double-stick tape.

Game Pieces

Step 6: Cut the wire into five ½" (1.3 cm) pieces. Hold one wire behind the holes in one button (Figure 2). With the thread doubled, make one lark's head knot near one end of the wire and bring the needle and thread up through one hole in the button, pulling the wire against the back of the button.

Step 7: String 12 size 11°s, take the needle down through the other hole, and secure the thread to the other side of the wire on the back of the button. Pass through the loop of beads and the holes of the button two more times. (Figure 3.)

Step 8: Repeat Step 3 to embellish the loop with "frothy fringe" (Figure 4).

Step 9: Repeat Steps 6–8 for all buttons.

Step 10: Trim the small squares and ovals of Ultrasuede to the size of the back of the buttons and glue in place to cover the wires and threads.

Pouch

Step 11: To miter the top flap of the pouch, measure down each long side of the remaining piece of Ultrasuede, and mark the fabric with the chalk 2½" (6.5 cm) from one short end. Draw a line at a 45-degree angle from these marked side edges toward the center of the short end; trim along the chalk line. Trim the Ultrasuede ½" (1.3 cm) from the tip of the flap. To create the pocket, fold up the untrimmed short end 3¼" (8.5 cm).

Step 12: Using size 11°s, add a picot edging around all edges of the Ultrasuede, joining the sides of the pocket where the Ultrasuede overlaps: Hiding the knot inside the pocket, bring a single knotted thread up through the fabric layers close to the bottom left edge, pick up 1 bead, and pass through both thicknesses of fabric from back to front. Pass back through the bead. *Pick up 2 beads and pass through the fabric from back to front, just under one bead's width away. Pass back through the last bead added. Being sure to pick up enough fabric to make the picot edging secure but not so much the stitches show, continue from * until the side and bottom edges of the bag have been secured. (Figure 5.)

Step 13: Repeat Step 3 to embellish the picot edging with "frothy fringe" along all sides except the top edge of the pocket (Figure 6).

Step 14: Making small holes in the Ultrasuede, if needed, and using the jump ring, attach the charm 2" (5 cm) below the tip of the flap.

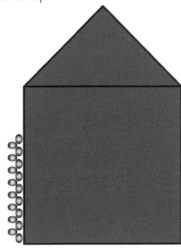

Figure 5

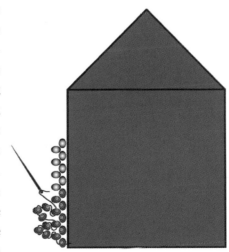

Figure 6

Positively Pretty Poinsettias

Bobbie Yoakum

This project is typically offered during Poppy Field Bead Company's fall schedule because of the holiday appeal of the poinsettia. However, with a simple change of color you'll have eye-catching flowers for any season. Bobbie originally chose tubular two-drop peyote for this project to add variety to her class schedule, and to her surprise, the stitch works up quickly—a good thing if dinner for twelve is on the menu.

Materials
5 g matte green silver-lined size 11° Japanese seed beads
5 g red silver-lined size 11° Japanese seed beads
8 g gold silver-lined size 11° Japanese seed beads
Size D beading thread in color to complement beads
Beeswax

Tools
Size 10 beading needle

Technique
Peyote stitch

Finished Size
1¾" (4.5 cm) poinsettia; 1½" (3.8 cm) diameter ring

TIP Keep Beads Still
✔ To keep the beads from sliding around when working tubular two-drop peyote stitch, slip the first rows of beads on a cardboard paper towel roll.
—Poppy Field Bead Company

Base

Step 1: Lightly wax 7' (2 m) of thread and leaving a 12" (30.5 cm) tail, string 3 green size 11°s. Tie the working thread and tail with a square knot to form a circle.

Step 2: Working counterclockwise, string 2 red size 11°s, pass through the first green size 11°, string 2 red size 11°s, pass through the second green size 11°, string 2 red size 11°s, and pass through the third green size 11°. Step up into the first red size 11°. (Figure 1.)

Figure 1

this project is from

Poppy Field Bead Company

**2531 Jefferson NE, Ste. 140
Albuquerque, NM 87110
(505) 880-8695
beadfield@poppyfield.com
www.poppyfield.com**

Beaders won't find extravagant displays or distracting signs at Poppy Field Bead Company—owner Margo Field prefers a "no frills" approach to her shop and presents beads so that they make a statement of their own. And what a statement! Margo, a prolific bead artist and teacher best known for her nature-themed artwork, opened Poppy Field more than ten years ago. A seed beader at heart, she carries a full line of size 11° and 15° Japanese seed beads, most of the Delica line, and a wide assortment of Czech glass beads.

The focus of the shop is on instruction: although peyote stitch is Margo's favorite stitch, she offers a variety of on-site beading classes where Margo and her staff pass along their knowledge and enthusiasm for the craft. With the recent addition of loomwork specialist and artist Bobbie Yoakum to the Poppy Field staff, Margo now has the time to travel and teach beading workshops around the world.

"The main reason that I teach beadwork to others is because I feel that everyone has a creative spirit in them that needs to be nourished," Margo says. "All of my students are artists to the best of their abilities and desires. Teaching beadwork is a way of learning about myself and others. I am a much happier and fulfilled person today than I was before I found beads."

In addition to the classes already available, Margo offers a "wish list" so that students can help schedule the types of classes they would like to take. Stop by to schedule a lesson—you won't want to miss the strong and rich creative spirit housed in this inviting and relaxed shop.

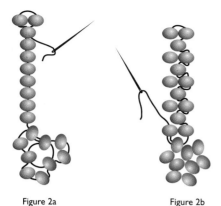

Figure 2a

Figure 2b

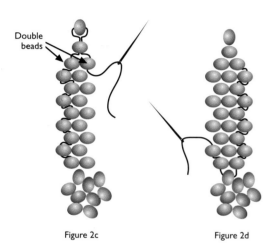

Double beads

Figure 2c

Figure 2d

Petal

Step 3: Work the petal in red size 11°s. String 10 beads and pass back through the eighth bead (Figure 2a). Working down the right side and moving toward the base, peyote stitch 4 beads; the fourth bead will be centered over the petal base bead. Pass through the base bead and the first bead strung in this Step. (Figure 2b.) Working up the left side and moving toward the tip, peyote stitch four times with 4 beads. The thread should exit out of the top right double bead created in Figure 1. String 2 beads, pass back through the first bead just added, and through the second double bead to the lower right. (Figure 2c.) Working down the right side and moving toward the base, peyote stitch 4 beads. Take the thread through the base bead and two beads on the left side. (Figure 2d.)

Step 4: Working on the left side and moving toward the tip, peyote stitch 3 beads. Take the thread through the two beads along the upper left side, cross over from one of the double beads at the top to the other double bead and down the beads along the top right side. Working on the right side and moving toward the base, peyote stitch 3 beads. Continue the thread through the two beads along the bottom right side, and through two base beads to start another petal or leaf. (Figure 2e.)

Step 5: Repeat Steps 3–4 for a total of six petals.

Leaves

Step 6: Work the leaf in green size 11°s. Begin a new waxed thread, exiting out of a green size 11° in the base. String 12 beads and pass back through the tenth bead. (Figure 3a.) Working on the right side and moving toward the base, peyote stitch a total of 5 beads. The fifth bead will be centered over the green base bead. Taking the thread through the opposite side of the base bead does this. Continue up through the first bead on the lower left side. (Figure 3b.)

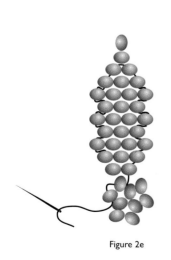

Figure 2e

Figure 3a

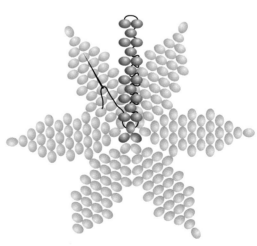

Figure 3b

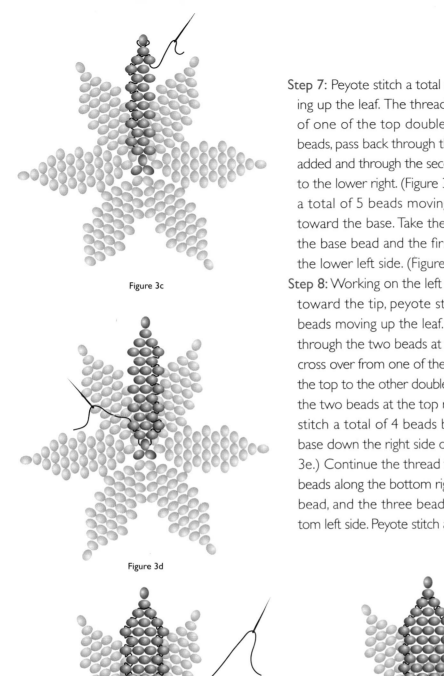

Figure 3c

Figure 3d

Step 7: Peyote stitch a total of 5 beads moving up the leaf. The thread should exit out of one of the top double beads. String 2 beads, pass back through the first bead just added and through the second double bead to the lower right. (Figure 3c.) Peyote stitch a total of 5 beads moving down the leaf toward the base. Take the thread through the base bead and the first two beads on the lower left side. (Figure 3d.)

Step 8: Working on the left side and moving toward the tip, peyote stitch a total of 4 beads moving up the leaf. Take the thread through the two beads at the top left side, cross over from one of the double beads at the top to the other double bead and down the two beads at the top right side. Peyote stitch a total of 4 beads back toward the base down the right side of the leaf. (Figure 3e.) Continue the thread through the two beads along the bottom right side, the base bead, and the three beads along the bottom left side. Peyote stitch a total of 3 beads moving toward the top of the leaf. Bring the thread through the three beads along the upper left side of the leaf, across the double beads at the top, and down the three beads along the upper right side. Peyote stitch a total of 3 beads moving toward the base. (Figure 3f.) Bring the thread through the beads along the lower right side, across the double beads near the base, and upward through the beads along the lower left side.

Step 9: Working on the left side of the leaf and moving toward the top, peyote stitch 2 beads. Bring the thread through the beads along the upper left side, across the double beads at the top, and down the beads along the upper right side. Moving toward the base, peyote stitch 2 beads. Bring the thread through the beads along the lower right side and two base beads. (Figure 3g.)

Step 10: Repeat Steps 6–9 for a total of three leaves. The leaves should be positioned under the petals when the poinsettia is finished.

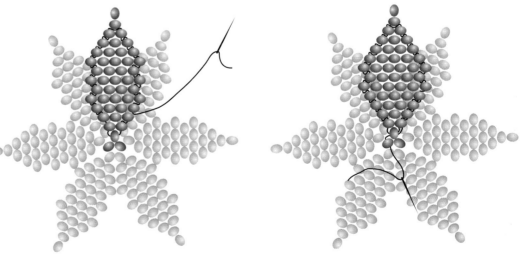

Figure 3e

Figure 3f

Figure 3g

Center

Step 11: Starting with any green size 11° of the base bead, consider this bead 1. Continue numbering the base beads in a clockwise manner from 1–9. Begin a new thread, exiting out of bead 1. (Figure 4.)

Step 12: String 2 gold size 11°s and cross the center to bead 3. Pass through bead 3, back through the two gold size 11°s, and through beads 1 and 9. (Figure 5.)

Step 13: String 3 gold size 11°s beads and cross the center to bead 5. Pass through beads 5 and 4, back through the three gold size 11°s, and through beads 9 and 8. (Figure 6.)

Step 14: String 2 gold size 11°s and cross the center to bead 6. Pass through bead 6, back through the two gold size 11°s, and through bead 8. Position the thread so that it is coming out a lower edge bead, close to the base of a petal. (Figure 7.)

Step 15: Secure the petals to each other by connecting a side bead near the base of each petal to the corresponding bead on the adjacent petal. Working to the left, follow the thread path through the petal to the next edge bead. (Figure 8.)

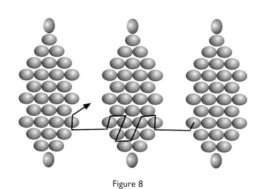

Figure 8

Ring

Step 16: To work tubular two-drop peyote, string 80 gold size 11°s (these beads will become the first and second row). Leaving a 4" (10 cm) tail, tie the working thread and tail with a square knot to form a circle.

Step 17: *String 2 green size 11°s, skip two gold 11°s of the ring, and pass through the next two gold 11°s (Figure 9a). Repeat from * around. Step up through the first two green size 11°s you added in this round (Figure 9b).

Step 18: Continue adding two-drop rows in the following color sequence: peyote two rows with gold size 11°s, two rows with green size 11°s, two rows with red size 11°s, two rows with green size 11°s, eleven rows with gold size 11°s, two rows with green size 11°s, two rows with red size 11°s, two rows with green size 11°s, and two rows with gold size 11°s.

Step 19: Attach the poinsettia to the ring: sew the leaves to the ring by having the thread attached to the leaf go through some beads in the ring and back through beads in the leaf. Continue this process until all the leaves are secured to the ring, following the thread path in the leaves and ring so that the thread won't show.

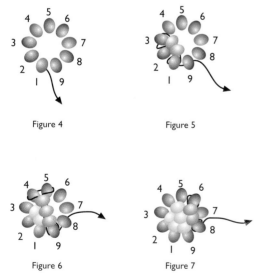

Figure 4

Figure 5

Figure 6

Figure 7

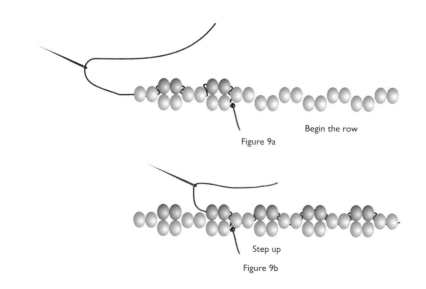

Begin the row

Figure 9a

Step up

Figure 9b

Feelin' Free

●●●●●●●●

Cynthia Hoglund

The focal point of this irresistible necklace is completely encrusted with beautiful beads. Mix things up by using your favorite crystals, pearls, or metal beads for a completely different look—no two beaded beads will ever be alike. For a more versatile look, replace the silk cording with a plain beading wire or a chain necklace.

Materials
- 5 g teal transparent size 11° Japanese seed beads
- 5 g teal white-lined size 11° Japanese seed beads
- 90–120 assorted 2–10mm semiprecious beads, freshwater pearls, crystals, metallic beads, and glass cubes
- 2 silver 13×7mm beads
- 1 pair of sterling silver 3mm leather ends
- Size D beading thread in color to complement beads
- 15½" (39.5 cm) strand of teal hand-dyed silk cord
- Clear nail polish

Tools
- Size 10 beading needle

Techniques
- Ladder stitch, tubular herringbone stitch

Finished size
- 15" (38 cm)

this project is from

Magpies Inc.

207 E. State St.
Cherry Valley, IL 61016
(815) 332-1890
robin.magpie@gmail.com
www.magpiesinc.com

Looking for an adventure? Take a trip to Magpies, located in a nineteenth-century mercantile building in the charming village of Cherry Valley, Illinois. But be warned: once you pull up a chair, the inviting hometown atmosphere may have you looking for a permanent residence!

Every month of the year, beaders find classes for all skill levels in disciplines including stringing, stitching, chain making, wire wrapping, Art Clay Silver, and more. The shop is always lively with special events like trunk shows and Beader's Night Out (where everyone is encouraged to bring their unfinished projects), a monthly beading contest with themes like Tip Toe Through the Tulips or Dog Days of Summer, and demonstrations on subjects like loomwork, crochet, lost wax casting, and more. Magpies also features a large lending library of books and magazines on a wide array of interests.

Owner Robin Walter says that if the heart of Magpies is their classes, the soul of Magpies is their employees. "Our employees volunteer for community service and teach beading classes at our local community college," she says. "They are always willing to help with an idea, sit down to give an impromptu lesson, or just lend a listening ear."

With a wide selection of semiprecious beads, freshwater pearls, silver beads and findings, Czech glass, vintage glass beads and buttons, Art Clay Silver, and a full line of beading tools, what else could a beader wish for? Bring your creativity and a friend and spend the day at Magpies.

Step 1: Join 8 transparent size 11°s using ladder stitch.

Step 2: To create the first row of the core, join the last bead to the first bead using ladder stitch (Figure 1).

Step 3: Work tubular herringbone stitch: String 2 transparent size 11°s and pass down through the bead directly to the left of the bead that the thread is exiting. *Pass the needle up through the bead to the left of the bead you just exited. String 2 transparent size 11°s and pass down through the bead to the left. Repeat from * until the row is complete. (Figure 2.) Pass the needle up through the bead to the left of the bead you just exited, and step up through the bead directly above it. Continue until the core is 2" (5 cm) long.

Step 4: To embellish the core: Bring the needle out of any core bead, string 1 white-lined size 11°, 1 assorted bead, and 1 white-lined size 11°. Pass the needle through the nearest core bead.

Step 5: Repeat Step 4 until the entire core is covered. (Figure 3.)

Step 6: String the cord with one end of the leather crimp, run the cord back through the crimp leaving just a small amount of the core exposed, and crimp the end. Tie a knot in the cord 6" (15 cm) from the end of the crimp, string 1 silver bead, the beaded bead, 1 silver bead, and tie a knot in the silk. Attach the remaining leather crimp on the other end of the cord in the same manner.

Figure 1

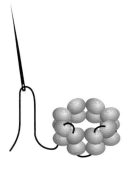

Figure 2

Figure 3

Seed Bead Snowflake Buttons

Charlene Abrams

These charming covered buttons are wonderfully versatile beading projects—once you've mastered the netting technique, they stitch up in no time and have a multitude of uses. Affix them to your favorite hand-knitted cardigan or hat, string them on beading wire for a truly original necklace or bracelet, or thread the button shank with an elastic hair band for a unique hairpiece.

Materials
2 g each of light green opaque (A), tan opaque (B), amber AB (C), dark green opaque (D), and matte crystal (E) size 11° Japanese seed beads
Size D beading thread in color to complement beads
1 size 45 (1⅛" [2.9 cm] in diameter) Dritz snap-in half-ball cover button
1 piece brown 3×3" (20.5×20.5 cm) fabric

Tools
Size 12 beading needle

Technique
Netting

Finished Size
1¼" (3.2 cm) in diameter

Note: Dritz snap-in half-ball cover buttons are available at fabric and craft stores or online resources.

TIPS

Play with Color
✔ When making additional buttons, mix up the colors. Pick a mixture of beads including contrasting colors, light and dark, and coordinating colors. Keep in mind that if your beads are too close in value and hue, the pattern will not be distinct. If using any silver-lined beads for the covered buttons, these work well as color A, as they are taller than beads with other finishes and may distort the pattern if used elsewhere.

Skip a Step
✔ Although Japanese seed beads are generally very regular in size, there may be some variation that causes your netted snowflake to be larger than you wish and to not fit snugly on the covered button. In this case, skip Step 9. In Step 11, join sets of 5D to the fabric by passing through the center 3Ds in each set of 5D.

—Lady Bug Beads

this project is from

Lady Bug Beads

7616 Big Bend Blvd.
St. Louis, MO 63119
(314) 644-6140
ladybugbeads@sbcglobal.net
www.ladybugbeads.net

Susan Rabbitt credits her mother with giving her the confidence to open Lady Bug Beads. "My mother's philosophy in life was, 'If you want to do something, do it today because you don't know what tomorrow will bring,'" Susan says. "It took me fifty years to believe that, but now I do. I didn't think there were enough beads in St. Louis, and thankfully I was right!"

Susan and her husband, Mike, operate the store, which opened in August 2003 in a 3,000-square-foot building in western St. Louis. They have created an inviting atmosphere where beaders linger for hours: an open floor plan, daylight-colored bulbs for accurate color matching, ample counter space for working on projects, and beads in dishes, trays, martini glasses, tubes, and hanks as far as the eye can see. Although Susan's passion is seed beads, Lady Bug Beads also stocks a selection of pearls, stones, Swarovski crystals, and semiprecious, Bali and Thai silver, Czech, and pressed-glass beads.

Stop by for a bead social any Tuesday evening, or bring in your coffee club or scout troop for a special party or event. Each spring and fall Lady Bug Beads sponsors the Bead Art and Jewelry Show in their parking lot, a great venue for customers to find new clients and meet local artists.

Every month beaders find new classes focusing on seed bead stitching, Precious Metal Clay, wire-working, finishing techniques, and more. On-the-spot education in earrings, necklaces, and bracelets is complimentary. "We're always eager to share our addiction and enthusiasm with new beaders," Susan says. "Some of our customers just stop by because they need a shot of inspiration; we hope you'll stop by too."

Step 1: String 6A. Leaving a 6" (15 cm) tail, knot the tail and working thread to create a circle and pass through the first bead.

Step 2: *String 1A and pass through the next bead in the circle. Repeat from * five more times to complete the round (6 new beads total). Pass through the first A added in this Step. (Figure 1.)

Step 3: *String 3B, pass through the next A. Repeat from * five more times to complete the round (6 sets of 3 new beads total). Pass through the first 2B added in this Step. (Figure 2.)

Step 4: *String 1C, 1D, 1E, 1D, 1C, and pass through the center B of the next point. Repeat from * five times to complete the round (6 sets of 5 new beads total). Pass through the first C and D added in this Step. (Figure 3.)

Step 5: *String 1E, 1B, 1E, and pass through the next D. String 3C and pass through the next D. Repeat from * five times to complete the round (6 sets of 6 new beads total). Pass through the first E and B added in this Step. (Figure 4.)

Step 6: *String 1B, 1A, 1D, skip 1C of the previous round, and pass through the next C. String 1D, 1A, 1B, and pass through the next B. Repeat from * to complete the round (6 sets of 6 new beads total). Pass through the first B and the A added in this Step. (Figure 5.)

Step 7: *String 5A and pass through the next A and B. String 4B, pass through the first B just added, then pass through the next B and A. Repeat from * five times to complete the round (6 sets of 9 beads total). Pass through the first 3A added in this Step. (Figure 6.)

Step 8: To begin constructing the framework that will hold the netted beads onto the

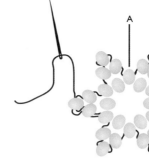

Figure 1

Figure 2

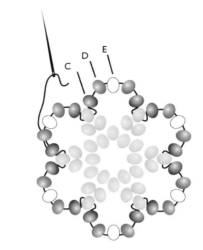

Figure 3

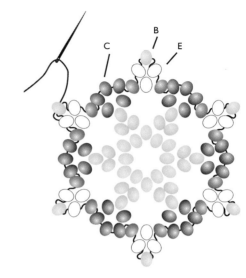

Figure 4

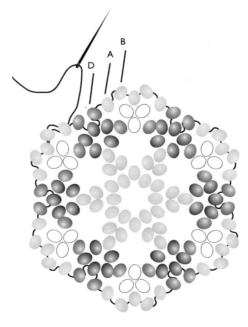

Figure 5

Figure 6

button form, *string 5D, pass through the A at the tip of the next point. String 5B and pass through the center (third) A of the previous row's set of 5A. Repeat from * five times to complete the round (6 sets of 10 beads total). Pass through the 3D added in this Step. (Figure 7.)

Step 9: *String 4D and pass through the center (third) D of the previous row's 5D. Repeat from * eleven times to complete the round (12 sets of 4 new beads). Pass through the first 3D added in this Step. (Figure 8.)

Step 10: Pull the thread tight (to form a cupped shape with the beads). Cover the half-ball cover button with the fabric according to manufacturer's directions. Insert the button cover, easing the beadwork around it. Ensure your tension is tight by pulling the thread tight.

Step 11: When attaching the beadwork to the button, sew through some of the fabric on the back of the button, very close to the metal center: take a stitch between 2–3 beads long and pass through the center 2D of the next 4D, keeping your thread tension tight. Repeat around the button until the center 2D of all 12 sets of 4D are attached to the button. Weave in the working thread and the tail, tie a few half hitch knots, and trim the threads close.

VARIATION For a smaller button that is ⅞" (2.2 cm) in diameter, use one size 30 (¾" [2 cm] in diameter) Dritz snap-in half-ball cover buttons in place of the size 45 half-ball cover buttons and repeat Steps 1–11 using size 15° beads in place of the size 11° beads.

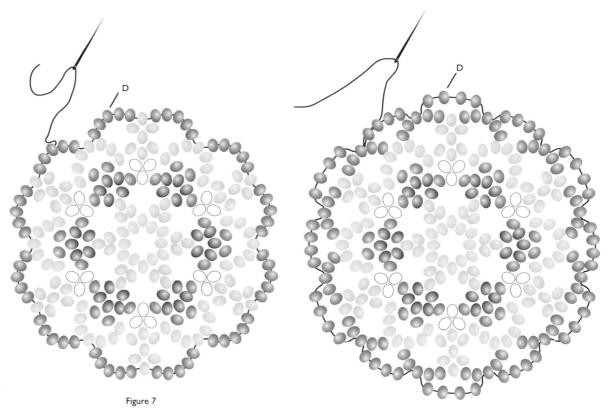

Figure 7

Figure 8

Seed Bead Snowflake Buttons variation

Beading Basics

You probably have some beading skills up your sleeve, but in case you'd like to brush up, here's a refresher course in the basics. This section covers all the general terms and techniques any beader needs to create all the projects in this book. While we can't list all the beads, materials, and tools available on the market, it's a great resource to get you started beading.

Pass Through vs Pass Back Through

Pass through means to move your needle in the same direction that the beads have been strung. Pass back through means to move your needle in the opposite direction.

Finishing and Starting New Threads

Tie off your old thread when it's about 4" (10 cm) long by making a simple knot between beads. Pass through a few beads and pull tight to hide the knot. Weave through a few more beads and trim the thread close to the work. Start the new thread by tying a knot between beads and weaving through a few beads. Pull tight to hide the knot. Weave through several beads until you reach the place to resume beading.

Tension Bead

A tension bead (or stopper bead) temporarily holds your work in place. To make one, string a bead larger than those you are working with, then pass through the bead one or more times, making sure not to split your thread. The bead will be able to slide along, but will still provide tension to work against

when you're beading the first two rows.

Gluing

Place a sparing amount of glue on knots to secure them (we recommend G-S Hypo Cement or clear nail polish), or use enough glue to completely secure beads to a surface (E6000, Terrifically Tacky Tape). Allow any glue to dry thoroughly before continuing. Seal large glue-beaded surfaces with Mod Podge.

Bead Types

Bakelite beads and buttons are vintage treasures made of an early nonflammable plastic from the 1920s–1940s. Bakelite was used to form many things other than beads, including clocks, kitchen items, and jewelry boxes.

Bone and horn beads are handmade beads that usually come from Indonesia and the Philippines; they're created from the bone or horns of working animals such as goats, camels, and cattle. Initially white, bone beads can be dyed any color.

Cane glass beads (also called furnace glass) are colorful handmade glass beads made from long glass canes that have been blown and pulled from a large mass of molten glass resting on the edge of a blow pipe.

Ceramic beads are handmade clay beads that have been fired at a high temperature. The beads can be glazed, resulting in a shiny finish and many colors, or left natural, resulting in a matte brown finish.

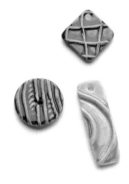

Crystal beads most often come from the Swarovski company in Austria. Crisp facets and a clean finish on these leaded glass beads create their brilliant sparkle. Crystals come in several shapes (round, bicone, drop, and cubes) and nearly one hundred colors. Use durable beading wire with crystal beads because their sharp edges can cause extra wear.

Czech pressed-glass beads are colorful beads from the Czech Republic made by pressing glass into a variety of molds. The beads are also called Czech glass and come in shapes that range from simple rounds, ovals, and squares to leaves, flowers, animals, and more.

Dichroic glass beads are handmade glass beads made with a special kind of glass that is thinly layered with several different metals that produce different colors depending how the light reflects off of it.

Enamel beads are metal (usually brass or copper) beads that have been painted or baked with enamel, which gives them a glossy, smooth, colorful surface.

Fire-polished beads are Czech glass beads that start as rounds and are then hand- or machine-faceted to catch the light. These beads come in every color imaginable and are available with several different added surface finishes that create extra sparkle.

Fused-glass beads are handmade beads created with pieces of glass that have been fused together in a kiln. A mandrel is inserted between the pieces before they are melted to create a hole for beading.

Lampworked beads are artistic handmade beads created with hot glass spun onto a mandrel over a flame. Since some lampworked beads can be exceptionally heavy, use stringing materials appropriate for their weight.

Metal beads vary in type of metal, shape, and size.

- **Bali silver beads** are handmade sterling silver beads made in Bali, Indonesia.

- **Gold-filled beads** are those in which $\frac{1}{10}$ of 12k gold is applied to the surface of brass or another base material. The resulting bead is very strong.

- **Pewter beads** are a dull silver color and are a less expensive alternative to other metal beads. Make sure the pewter is lead free.

- **PMC (Precious Metal Clay) beads** are handmade from a claylike substance that can be rolled, formed, and treated like clay; when fired, PMC becomes 99.9 percent fine silver.

• *Silver and 18k gold-plated beads* are created by an electroplating process. A very thin layer of silver or gold is applied to another type of metal like brass or copper.

• *Sterling silver beads* are a mix of silver and copper. To be sold legally as sterling, the percentages must be 92.5 percent pure silver and 7.5 percent copper. While some people have allergic skin reactions when wearing less pure metal jewelry, most can wear sterling silver jewelry without such reactions.

• *Thai silver beads* are handmade in Thailand by the Karen hill tribe, who use old car parts as tools to make their beads. Thai silver is 99.5 to 99.9 percent fine silver.

• *Vermeil* (pronounced vehr-MAY) *beads* are made of sterling silver electroplated with gold.

Pearl beads come in several types and qualities. The projects in this book use both cultured freshwater and Swarovski crystal pearls.

• *Freshwater pearls* are cultured in inland lakes and rivers. The pearls are real pearls, as they are collected from oysters, but the irritant that formed the pearl was manually inserted. Therefore, they come in all sizes and shapes.

• *Crystal pearl beads* are made by the Swarovski company. They are crystals that have been coated with a pearl-like substance. Because crystal is the core of these pearls, they have the weight of real pearls, a benefit over other imitation pearls.

Polymer clay beads are colorful handmade plasticine (a claylike substance made of synthetic materials) beads that are fired at low temperatures. Polymer clay is often used to make colorful beads and pendants in all sorts of patterns, shapes, and sizes.

Raku beads are handmade clay beads that are fired at very high temperatures, resulting in brilliant colors from the applied glazes.

Resin beads are transparent, very durable synthetic beads that come in bright, candylike colors. Handmade in Java, Indonesia, these beads come in several shapes, but are not always uniform in size.

Seed beads are tiny pieces of a thin, long glass cane that are melted slightly or tumbled to round the edges. Seed beads come in several different finishes, such as iridescent, matte, satin, silver-lined, and transparent.

• *Cylinder beads* (brand names: Delicas, Tohos, and Magnificas) are perfectly cylindrical beads with thin walls and large holes. They come in two sizes—regular and large, which approximate a size 11° seed bead and a size 8° seed bead. The degree mark next to the size is called an "ought," and is a traditional beading term/symbol; its origin is obscure.

• *Czech seed beads* come on hanks, are shaped like tiny donuts, and are slightly irregular. They are sized from 20° to 6° (the smaller the number, the larger the bead). Charlottes are size 13° beads with a facet that makes them sparkle.

• *Japanese seed beads* are sold in tubes or by the kilo and are shaped more like cylinders, giving them larger holes. They come in 6°, 8°, 11°, and 14/15° sizes (again, the smaller the number, the larger the bead).

Semiprecious stone beads, whether naturally made by the earth or sea creatures, or man-made, are available in hundreds of varieties. They come in all sizes and shapes, but generally they are polished and faceted, donut-shaped, rough-cut, or chips. These beads are usually heavy, so use a strong beading wire when stringing them.

Venetian glass beads are beads handmade on the island of Murano and in Venice, Italy. The sparkle from these beads is due to a mixture of metals added to the glass and often a central layer of glass wrapped in silver, gold, or platinum.

Vintage beads are just that: old beads utilizing glass materials and/or techniques that are no longer available or commonly used.

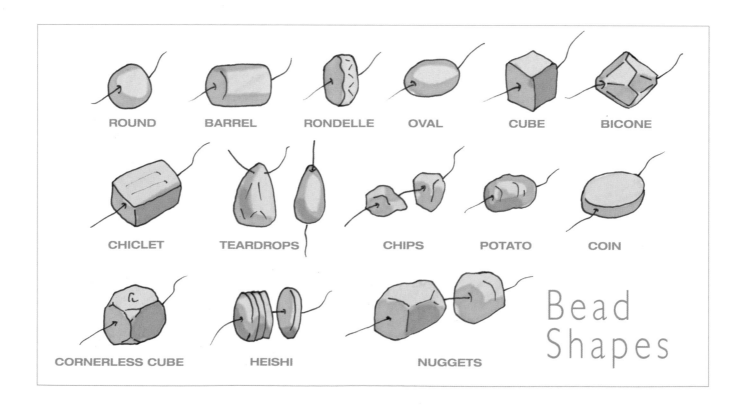

ROUND BARREL RONDELLE OVAL CUBE BICONE

CHICLET TEARDROPS CHIPS POTATO COIN

CORNERLESS CUBE HEISHI NUGGETS

Bead Shapes

Stringing

Stringing is a technique in which you use a beading wire, needle and thread, or other material to gather beads into a strand.

Stringing Materials

Beading wire is nylon-covered strands of steel, available in colors and widths—use .024 for large, abrasive beads; .019 for crystals and small lampworked beads; and .014 for small, lightweight beads such as pearls. Ironically, the more strands of steel in a wire, the more supple it is. Secure beading wire to findings with crimp tubes.

Leather, suede, waxed linen, and silk cords come in many colors and sizes. Shapes range from round lacing to flat ribbon. Beads can be strung and knotted directly on cords, or you can mix cords with other stringing materials and findings for more design options.

Beading threads such as Nymo, C-Lon, and Silamide are strong synthetic threads suitable for stringing, but they're most commonly used for on- and off-loom beadwork.

Tools

Crimping pliers squeeze and secure a crimp tube onto beading wire and are available in three sizes: micro for 1×1mm crimp tubes, regular for 2mm and 2×3mm crimp tubes, and mighty for 3×3mm crimp tubes.

Crimping pliers

Millimeter Bead Size Chart

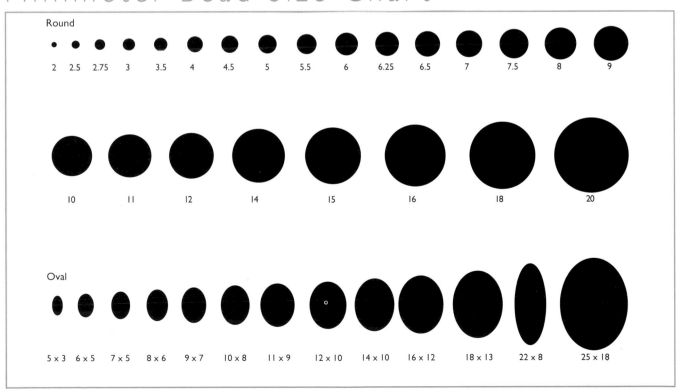

Round

2   2.5   2.75   3   3.5   4   4.5   5   5.5   6   6.25   6.5   7   7.5   8   9

10   11   12   14   15   16   18   20

Oval

5 x 3   6 x 5   7 x 5   8 x 6   9 x 7   10 x 8   11 x 9   12 x 10   14 x 10   16 x 12   18 x 13   22 x 8   25 x 18

Round-nose pliers have tapered cylindrical jaws for making loops. Positioning the wire at different points of the jaws yields several different sizes of loops.

Round-nose pliers

Chain- and flat-nose pliers have flat, tapered jaws for gripping and bending wire and for flattening crimp beads. Be sure that the inside of your flat- or chain-nose pliers are smooth so that they don't mar your crimp tubes or wire.

Chain-nose pliers

Wire cutters have sharp blades that cut wire flush and leave no burrs.

Wire cutters

Crimping

Crimp tubes are seamless tubes of metal that come in several sizes, including 1×1mm, 2×2mm, 2×3mm, and 3×3mm. Ask your local bead shop or check on the websites of wire manufacturers to see which crimp tubes work best with your preferred size of wire. To use, string a crimp tube and pass the beading wire through the connection finding. Pass back through the tube, leaving a short tail. Use the back notch of the crimping pliers to press the length of the tube down between the wires, enclosing them in separate chambers of the crescent shape. Rotate the tube 90° and use the front notch to fold the two chambers onto themselves, forming a clean cylinder. Trim the excess wire.

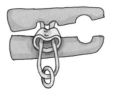

Crimp covers hide 2×2mm crimp tubes and give a professional finish. To place a crimp cover around the crimped tube, gently hold a crimp cover in the front notch of the crimping pliers. Insert the crimped tube and gently squeeze the pliers, encasing the tube inside the cover.

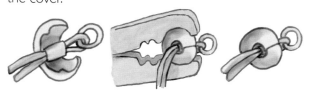

Findings

Findings—usually metal—are the clasps, connectors, and components that keep pieces together or add visual appeal. Following are the descriptions of popular findings.

Chain is links of soldered metal loops that act as a base for many jewelry projects. Connect beads and clasps to this finding with jump rings, split rings, or wirework.

Clasps connect the ends of necklaces or bracelets. Some have one loop for single-strand jewelry, others have two or more loops for multistranded pieces.

• *Box clasps* are shaped like a rectangular, square, or circular box on one end and have a bent metal tab on the other end that snaps into the box under its own tension. Many are decorated with beautiful designs and inlaid stones.

• *Buttons* with shanks are a great option for clasps and can also be incorporated into pieces as a focal point or design element.

• *Hook and eye clasps* are comprised of a J-shaped side and a loop side that hook into each other. This clasp requires tension to keep it closed, so it's best used with necklaces that have some weight.

• *S-hooks* are made up of an S-shaped wire permanently attached to a jump ring on one side; the S closes through a second jump ring on the other end of the piece. This clasp, like the hook and eye, depends on tension to keep it closed.

• *Toggle clasps* are made up of a bar on one side and a ring on the other. A good toggle clasp will not come apart on its own because the bar is long enough so that it must be turned and manually passed through the ring.

Crimp beads and tubes help to secure beading wire to clasps and connectors, or wherever you need to make a connection.

Crimp covers are shiny pieces of sterling silver or gold-filled metal that wrap around crimp tubes with the help of crimping pliers. They look like round beads and are a great design element.

Eye pins are straight pieces of wire with a loop on one end.

Head pins are straight pieces of wire with a small stopper at one end that are often used for making earrings or other dangles.

Jump rings are small circles of wire used to connect pieces of beadwork. To open, bend the ends away from each other laterally; do not pull the ends apart.

Separator bars keep the wires of multistranded jewelry separated and tidy. Use them by passing a thread or wire through each hole.

Split rings are shaped like tiny key rings. They are really doubled-up jump rings that create a secure attachment because they don't pull open.

Wireworking

Metal wire comes in many finishes and gauges, as well as many shapes (round, half-round, square, rectangular, triangular, twisted, etc.). The lower the gauge number, the thicker the wire. The hardness or softness of wire is called "temper." Most wire comes in dead-soft, half-hard, and hard tempers.

To form a **simple loop,** use flat-nose pliers to make a 90° bend at least ½" (1.3 cm) from the end of the wire. Use round-nose pliers to grasp the wire after the bend; roll the pliers toward the bend, but not past it, to preserve the 90° bend. Use your thumb to continue the wrap around the nose of the pliers. Trim the wire next to the bend. Open a simple loop by grasping each side of its

opening with a pair of pliers. Don't pull apart. Instead, twist in opposite directions so that you can open and close without distorting the shape.

To form a **wrapped loop,** begin with a 90° bend at least 2" (5 cm) from the end of the wire. Use round-nose pliers to form a simple loop with a tail overlapping the bend. Wrap the tail tightly down the neck of the wire to create a couple of coils. Trim the excess wire to finish. Make a thicker, heavier-looking wrapped loop by wrapping the wire back up over the coils, toward the loop, and trimming the wire at the loop.

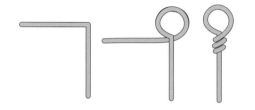

Link a wire wrapped loop to another loop by threading the wire through the previous loop before wrapping the neck of the new loop.

Dangles can be strung as they are, attached using jump rings, or linked onto other loops. Use a head pin to string the bead(s), then form a simple or wrapped loop.

Bails turn side-drilled beads, usually teardrops, into pendants. Center the bead on a 6" (15 cm) piece of wire. Bend both ends of the wire up the sides and across the top of the bead. Bend one end straight up at the center of the bead and wrap the other wire around it to form a few coils. Form a wrapped loop with the straight-up wire, wrapping it back down over the already-formed coils. Trim the excess wire.

To make a coil, use one hand to hold the end of your wire against a mandrel. With the other hand, wrap the wire around the mandrel in tight loops. To remove the coil, slide it off the mandrel and cut. Add vertical loops on either end to use the coil as is, or cut the coil at certain intervals to make jump rings or split rings.

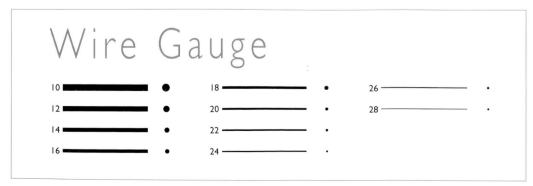

Wire Gauge

10	•	18	•	26	•
12	•	20	•	28	•
14	•	22	•		
16	•	24	•		

To start a spiral, make a small loop at the end of a wire with round-nose pliers. Enlarge the piece by holding on to the spiral with chain-nose pliers, pushing the wire over the previous coil with your thumb, and repositioning the wire in the chain-nose pliers as needed.

Knots

The **overhand knot** is the basic knot for tying off thread. It is not very secure, but helps to hold thread in place. Make a loop with the stringing material. Pass the cord that lies behind the loop over the front cord and through the loop. Pull tight.

The **square knot** is the classic sturdy knot for securing most stringing materials. First make an overhand knot, passing the right end over the left end. Next, make another overhand knot, this time passing the left end over the right end. Pull tight.

The **surgeon's knot** is very secure and therefore good for finishing off most stringing materials. Tie an overhand knot, right over left, but instead of one twist over the left cord, make at least two. Tie another overhand knot, left over right, and pull tight.

Half hitch knots may be worked with two or more strands—one strand is knotted over one or more other strands. Form a loop around the cord(s). Pull the end through the loop just formed and pull tight. Repeat for the length of cord you want to cover.

Lark's head knots are great for securing stringing material to another piece, such as a ring or a donut. Begin by folding the stringing material in half. Pass the fold through a ring or donut. Pull the ends through the loop created by the fold and pull tight.

Beading Needles

Beading needles are very fine, long (up to 3" [7.5 cm]) needles whose eyes are the same width as the rest of the needle—an important feature when you consider the added width of the stringing material. Beading needles work well for very small-holed beads like small seed beads, pearls, and some semi-precious stones. Because the eye size is so small, beading needles can be a challenge to thread. To make it easier, place the stringing material between the thumb and forefinger of your nondominant hand, allowing just a small amount of the end to peek out. Use your dominant hand to place the needle eye on the end and pull it through.

Big-eye needles come in 2¼" and 5" (5.5 and 12.5 cm) lengths and have pointed ends with a double wire down the center. They are the easiest needles to thread—simply separate the center wires, place the stringing material between, and allow the wires to collapse on themselves to capture the thread. These needles work well for fairly small-holed beads, and the 5" (12.5 cm) long version is especially for one-time use in stringing because you can easily see if you've strung your beads in the correct order.

Twisted wire needles are made of fine wire and feature a large loop on one end and a twisted shank on the other. You thread the stringing material through the loop and, as you pass the needle through a bead, the loop collapses to secure the stringing material. Twisted-wire needles are generally one-use and work well for small holed beads such as pearls.

Ladder Stitch

For a **single-needle ladder,** string 2 beads and pass through them again. String 1 bead. Pass through the last stitched bead and the one just strung. Repeat, adding one bead at a time and working in a figure-eight pattern.

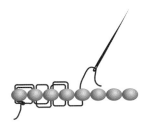

Brick Stitch

Begin by creating a foundation row in ladder stitch or using a secured thread. String 1 bead and pass under the closest exposed loop of the foundation row. Pass back through the same bead and continue, adding one bead at a time.

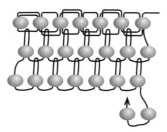

To decrease *within a row,* string 1 bead and skip a loop of thread on the previous row, passing under the second loop and back through the bead.

To increase *within a row,* work two stitches in the same space of the previous row.

Peyote Stitch

One-drop flat peyote stitch begins by stringing an even number of beads to create the first two rows. Begin the third row by stringing 1 bead and passing through the second-to-last bead of the previous rows. String another bead and pass through the fourth-to-last bead of the previous rows. Continue adding 1 bead at a time, passing over every other bead of the previous rows.

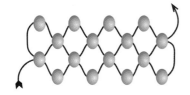

Two-drop flat peyote stitch is worked the same as above, but with 2 beads at a time instead of 1.

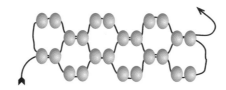

For *tubular peyote stitch,* string an even number of beads and make a foundation circle by passing through them two more times, exiting from the first bead strung. String 1 bead and pass through the third bead of the foundation circle. String 1 bead and pass through the fifth bead of the foundation circle. Continue adding 1 bead at a time, skipping over 1 bead of the first round, until you have added half the number of beads of the first round. Exit from the first bead of the second round. String 1 bead, pass through the second bead added in the second round, and pull the thread tight. String 1 bead and pass through the third bead added in the second round. Continue around, filling in the "spaces" 1 bead at a time. Exit from the first bead added in each round.

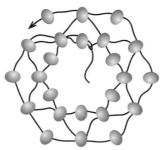

Right-Angle Weave (Single Needle)

String 4 beads and pass through them again to form the first unit. For the rest of the row, string 3 beads, pass through the last bead passed through in the previous unit, and the first two just strung; the thread path will resemble a figure eight, alternating directions with each unit. To begin the next row, pass through the last 3 beads strung to exit the side of the last unit. String 3 beads, pass through the last bead passed through, and the first bead just strung. *String 2 beads, pass through the next edge bead of the previous row, the last bead passed through in the previous unit, and the last 2 beads just strung. Pass through the next edge bead of the previous row, string 2 beads, pass through the last bead of the previous unit, the edge bead just passed through, and the first bead just strung. Repeat from * to complete the row, then begin a new row as before.

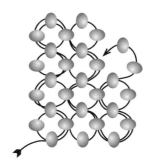

Bead Embroidery

For *backstitch embroidery,* begin by passing through the fabric, from wrong side to right side. String 4 beads. Lay the beads against the fabric and pass the needle down through the fabric, just past the fourth bead. Pass up through the fabric between the second and third beads and pass through the last 2 beads strung. String 4 beads and repeat.

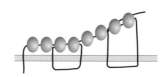

Picot edging makes a decorative and useful edge, and can be stitched along a folded edge, or to hold two edges together. Knot the thread and come up through the edge of the fabric, hiding your knot in the fold, or between the layers. String 3 beads and *make a stitch on the edge from back to front, about 1 bead's distance away. Pass back up through the last bead strung. String 2 beads and repeat from *.

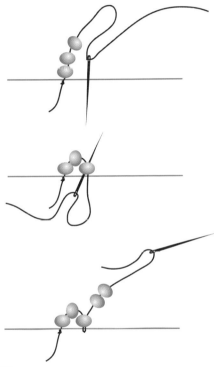

Fringe

For *basic fringe*, exit from your foundation row of beads or fabric. String a length of beads plus 1 bead. Skipping the last bead, pass back through all the beads just strung to create a fringe leg. Pass back into the foundation row or fabric.

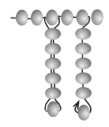

For *branch fringe*, start with a long but comfortable thread length. Knot the end and secure the knot in beadwork or on fabric. String beads the length of your desired finished fringe length. This will be the core of your branch fringe. Skip the last bead strung and pass back through 5 to 7 beads of the core. *String 5–7 beads. Skip the last bead strung and pass back through the rest of the beads just strung and 5 to 7 beads of the core. Repeat from * until you have made branches up the remaining length of your core.

For *looped fringe*, anchor your thread to the edge to be fringed. String a measured length of beads, form a loop, and take a stitch next to the first anchor spot. For each successive loop, string the same length of beads and pass the needle and thread through the previous loop to interlace the loops before anchoring the new loop to the edge.

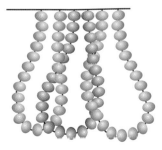

Weaving

Cut a length of weft thread about 36" (91.5 cm) long and tie it with a half-square knot onto an outside warp thread, leaving a 4–6" (10–15 cm) tail. (Tie onto the left warp thread if you are right-handed, the right warp thread if you are left-handed.) Thread the other end of the weft thread through a long beading needle. Thread the number of beads needed for the first row onto the weft thread and slide them down to the knot. Bring the beaded weft thread *under* the warp threads and push the beads up with your finger so there is one bead between each two warp threads. Hold the beads in place and pass back through all the beads, making sure that this time the weft thread passed *over* the warp threads. Repeat these steps for each row.

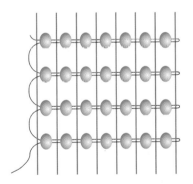

Adding weft thread. When you near the end of a weft thread, leave about a 6" (15 cm) tail at the end of a row; you'll weave the tail in when the loomwork is finished. Tie a new weft thread onto the outside warp as you did to begin. Leave a tail on this thread and weave it into the piece when you're finished.

Adapted with permission from books published by Interweave Press LLC.

Directory of Bead Shops

The following shops submitted projects for *Beader's Stash*.

Alaska

Alaska Bead Company
2217 E. Tudor Rd., Ste. 7
Anchorage, AK 99507
(907) 563-2323
orders@alaskabead.com

Rainbow House
PO Box 116
Aniak, AK 99557
(907) 675-4376

Gig's Beads 'N Things
1266 Ocean Dr., Ste. A
Homer, AK 99603
(907) 235-2244
info@gigsbeads.com
www.gigsbeads.com

Arizona

The Bead Museum
5754 W. Glenn Dr.
Glendale, AZ 85301
(623) 930-7395
www.thebeadmuseum.com

California

The San Gabriel Bead Company
325 E. Live Oak Ave.
Arcadia, CA 91006
(626) 447-7753
info@beadcompany.com
www.beadcompany.com

International Glass & Bead Company
317 W. First St.
Claremont, CA 91711
(909) 626-0877
info@glassandbeads.com
www.glassandbeads.com

Talisman Beads
214 F St.
Eureka, CA 95501
(707) 443-1509
talisman@northcoast.com
www.talismanbeads.us

The Hole Affair
46 Main St.
Jackson, CA 95642
(209) 257-1793
www.theholeaffair.com

Heart Bead
830 G St.
Kneeland, CA 95521
(707) 826-9577
info@heartbead.com
www.heartbead.com

Beads of Marin Inc.
8 Locust Ave.
Mill Valley, CA 94941
(415) 381-4364
info@beadsofmarin.com
www.beadsofmarin.com

General Bead
317 National City Blvd.
National City, CA 91950
(619) 336-0100
genbead@sbcglobal.net
www.genbead.com

Creative Castle
2321 Michael Dr.
Newbury Park, CA 91320
(805) 499-1377
www.creativecastle.com

The Bead Shop
158 University Ave.
Palo Alto, CA 94301
(650) 328-7925
janice@beadshop.com
www.beadshop.com

Farrin O'Connor Design Studios
146 W. Bellevue Dr.
Pasadena, CA 91105
(626) 796-5300
farrinoconnordesign@yahoo.com
www.farrinoconnordesign.com

Third Eye Beads & Gift Gallery
434 N. El Camino Real
San Clemente, CA 92672
(949) 366-0219

General Bead
637 Minna St.
San Francisco, CA 94103
(415) 255-2323
genbead@sbcglobal.net
www.genbead.com

Beadissimo
1051 Valencia St.
San Francisco, CA 94110
(415) 282-2323
info@beadissimo.com
www.beadissimo.com

Legendary Beads
2725 Santa Rosa Ave.
Santa Rosa, CA 95407
(707) 569-0338
www.legendarybeads.com

Bead Depot Etc.
112 E. F St. #E
Tehachapi, CA 93561
(661) 822-5986
info@beaddepotetc.com
www.beaddepotetc.com

The Beading Place
604 El Camino Real
Tustin, CA 92780
(714) 832-7185
info@thebeadingplace.com
www.thebeadingplace.com

Colorado

The Bead Cache
3307 S. College Ave., Ste. 105
Fort Collins, CO 80525
(970) 224-4322

Purple Mountain Beads
4409 E. Prospect Rd.
Fort Collins, CO 80525
(970) 221-0809

Connecticut

Beadecked Bead Shoppe
35 N. Main St.
Southington, CT 06409
(860) 276-0475
info@beadster.com
www.beadster.com

Florida

Beadful Things
710-5 Pondella Rd.
North Fort Myers, FL 33903
(239) 652-0602

Bead Dreams
849 Sand Lake Rd.
Orlando, FL 32809
(407) 251-5050
www.beaddreamsinc.com

Buttons, Bangles & Beads
415 Corey Ave.
St. Pete Beach, FL 33706
(727) 363-4332
contact@buttonsbanglesandbeads.com
www.buttonsbanglesandbeads.com

Georgia

Beads by Design
585 Cobb Pkwy. S., Ste. L
Marietta, GA 30060
(770) 425-3909

Illinois

Magpies Inc.
207 E. State St.
Cherry Valley, IL 61016
(815) 332-1890
robin.magpie@gmail.com
www.magpiesinc.com

The Galena Bead Bar
109 N. Main St.
Galena, IL 61036
(815) 777-4080
galenabeadbar@msn.com
www.galenabeadbar.com

Bead in Hand
145 Harrison St.
Oak Park, IL 60304
(708) 848-1761
beadinhand@bigplanet.com
www.beadinhand.com

Indiana

Bead Angels Bead Shop
6419 N. Ferguson St.
Indianapolis, IN 46220
(317) 259-7677

Boca Loca Beads Inc.
872 Massachusetts Ave.
Indianapolis, IN 46204
(317) 423-2323
bocalocabeads@aol.com
www.bocalocabeadsinc.com

Iowa

Bead Haven
3260 Southgate Place SW, Ste. 1
Cedar Rapids, IA 52404
(319) 247-2323
beadhaven@hotmail.com
www.beadhavenbeads.com

Massachusetts

Turquoise/String Beads
420 Quequechan St.
Fall River, MA 02723
(508) 677-1877
www.turquoise-stringbeads.com

Albion Beads
20 Albion St.
Wakefield, MA 01880
(781) 245-1377
albionbeads@aol.com
www.albionbeads.com

The Bead Tree
67 Blacksmith Shop Rd.
West Falmouth, MA 02574
(508) 548-4665
beadtree@aol.com
www.thebeadtree.com

Maryland

Beadazzled
501 N. Charles St.
Baltimore, MD 21201
(410) 837-2323
www.beadazzled.net

Maine

The Beadin' Path
15 Main St.
Freeport, ME 04032
(207) 865-4785
beads@beadinpath.com
www.beadinpath.com

Michigan

Brighton Beads and More
9850 E. Grand River
Brighton, MI 48116
(810) 844-0066
staff@brightonbeadsandmore.com
www.brightonbeadsandmore.com

Bead Works Inc.
32751 Franklin Rd.
Franklin, MI 48025
(248) 855-5230
beads@franklinbeadworks.com
www.franklinbeadworks.com

The Creative Fringe LLC
210 Washington Ave.
Grand Haven, MI 49417
(616) 296-0020
stacy@thecreativefringe.com
www.thecreativefringe.com

Bead Culture
180 W. Michigan Ave.
Jackson, MI 49201
(517) 841-9173
www.beadculture.com

Regal Beader
3330 Glade St.
Muskegon, MI 49444
(231) 733-9909

Minnesota
Bead Me Up!
7707 147th St. W.
Apple Valley, MN 55124
(952) 997-2324
info@bead-me-up.com
www.bead-me-up.com

Sweet Beads
17516 Minnetonka Blvd.
Minnetonka, MN 55345
(952) 473-9671
info@mysweetbeads.com
www.mysweetbeads.com

Insomniac Beads LLC
11255 Hwy. 55, Ste. 50
Plymouth, MN 55441
(952) 345-6697
insomniacbeads@yahoo.com
www.insomniacbeads.com

Nordic Gypsy Beads and Jewelry
20 Third St. SW
Rochester, MN 55902
(507) 288-2258
web@nordicgypsy.com
www.nordicgypsy.com

Missouri
Lady Bug Beads
7616 Big Bend Blvd.
St. Louis, MO 63119
(314) 644-6140
ladybugbeads@sbcglobal.net
www.ladybugbeads.net

North Carolina
Beadazzled
107 W. Chatham St.
Cary, NC 27511
(919) 465-3455
beadazzled@bellsouth.net
www.beadazzledcary.com

Ornamentea
509 N. West St.
Raleigh, NC 27603
(919) 834-8634
info@ornamentea.com
www.ornamentea.com

North Dakota
Urban Girl
208 E. Broadway Ave.
Bismarck, ND 58501
(701) 323-9222
info@urbangirlonline.com
www.urbangirlonline.com

New Hampshire
Castleander Beads & Crafts
99 Lowell Rd. #5
Hudson, NH 03051
(603) 594-0048
castleander@hotmail.com
www.castleander.com

Bead Gallery Inc.
100 N. Broadway
Salem, NH 03079
(603) 893-2517
www.beadgalleryinc.com

New Jersey
Timeless Treasures Inc.
438 Bloomfield Ave.
Montclair, NJ 07042
(973) 783-7878

New Mexico
Poppy Field Bead Company
2531 Jefferson NE, Ste. 140
Albuquerque, NM 87110
(505) 880-8695
beadfield@poppyfield.com
www.poppyfield.com

Beauty and the Beads Inc.
939 W. Alameda St.
Santa Fe, NM 87501
(505) 982-5234
beads@santafebeads.com
www.santafebeads.com

New York
Dana Rudolph and Company
209-211 River St.
Troy, NY 12180
(518) 273-4532
dana@danarudolph.com
www.danarudolph.com

Ohio
Saki Silver
362 Ludlow Ave.
Cincinnati, OH 45220
(513) 861-9626
orders@sakisilver.com
www.sakisilver.com

Meant to Bead
6536 W. Central Ave.
Toledo, OH 43617
(419) 842-8183
meant2bead@aol.com
www.meant2bead.com

Oregon
Planet Bead
244 E. Main St.
Hillsboro, OR 97123
(503) 615-8509
webmaster@planetbeadonline.com
www.planetbeadllc.com

Dava Bead and Trade
1815 NE Broadway
Portland, OR 97232
(503) 288-3991
davabead@integraonline.com
www.davabeadandtrade.com

Beadcats/Universal Synergetics
PO Box 2840
Wilsonville, OR 97070
(503) 625-7168
tomcat@beadcats.com
www.beadcats.com

Pennsylvania
EZBeads.com
Olde Ridge Village #10
Chadds Ford, PA 19317
(610) 558-0565
custserv@ezbeads.com
www.ezbeads.com

Blue Santa Beads
17 Northgate Village
Media, PA 19063
(610) 892-2847
bluesantabeads@aol.com

Tennessee
Land of Odds/Be Dazzled Beads
718 Thompson Ln., Ste. 123
Nashville, TN 37204
(615) 292-0610
oddsian@landofodds.com
www.landofodds.com

Texas
Beadoholique Too!
8658 Hwy. 6 N.
Houston, TX 77095
(281) 858-4505
www.beadoholique.net

Beadoholique Bead Shop
8220 Louetta #124
Spring, TX 77379
(281) 257-0510
www.beadoholique.net

Utah
String Beads
2223 S. Highland Dr.
Salt Lake City, UT 84106
(801) 487-1110
www.stringbeadsutah.com

Virginia
Studio Baboo
106 5th St. SE
Charlottesville, VA 22902
(434) 244-2905
studiobaboo@earthlink.net
www.studiobaboo.com

Beadazzled
Tyson's Corner Center 1
McLean, VA 22102
(703) 848-2323
www.beadazzled.net

Star's Beads Ltd.
139 A Church St. NW
Vienna, VA 22180
(703) 938-7018
www.starsbeads.com

Washington
The Bead Garden
400 Winslow Wy., Ste. 180
Bainbridge Island, WA 98110
(206) 855-4043
www.thebead-garden.com

Beads & Beyond
25 102nd Ave. NE
Bellevue, WA 98004
(425) 462-8992

The Bead Garden
3382 A NW Carlton Wy.
Silverdale, WA 98383
(360) 692-8899
www.thebead-garden.com

The Bead Factory
3019 Sixth Ave.
Tacoma, WA 98406
(253) 572-5529
info@thebeadfactory.com
www.thebeadfactory.com

Beadclub
17616 140th Ave. NE
Woodinville, WA 98072
(425) 949-1080
info@beadclub.com
www.beadclub.com

Ambrosia Bead Company
5110 Tieton Dr., Ste. 230
Yakima, WA 98908
(509) 972-3750
beads@ambrosiabeadcompany.com
www.ambrosiabeadcompany.com

Washington, D.C.
Beadazzled
1507 Connecticut Ave. NW
Washington, D.C. 20036
(202) 265-2323
beadhq@beadazzled.net
www.beadazzled.net

Wisconsin
Gossamer Wings Beads
1008 19th St. S.
La Crosse, WI 54601
(608) 788-8229
weddings@gossamerwingsdesigns.com
www.gossamerwingsdesigns.com

Bead Bin
414 Westgate Mall
Madison, WI 53711
(608) 274-0104

Wyoming
Sorrelli
45 S. Main St.
Sheridan, WY 82801
(307) 673-0844
lori@labeadsorrelli.com
www.labeadsorrelli.com

Canada
Beads of Colour
65 Main St.
Dundas, ON
Canada L8N 2P9
(905) 628-6886
debi@beadsofcolour.com
www.beadsofcolour.com

Holy Crow Beads
R.R. 1
Clarksburg, ON
Canada N0H 1J0
(519) 599-5697
info@holycrowbeads.com
www.holycrowbeads.com

Suzie Q Beads
1207 Tenth Ave. SE
Calgary, AB
Canada T2G 0W6
(403) 266-1202
suzieqbeads@shaw.ca
www.suzieqbeads.com

Ireland
Yellow Brick Road
8 Bachelors Walk
Dublin 1, Ireland
353 1873 0177
sales@yellowbrickroad.ie
www.yellowbrickroad.ie

Online
Bluewater Beads Inc.
(online only)
(615) 565-4945
www.bluewaterbeads.com

Index